THE
MAKING OF AMERICA
SERIES

SACRAMENTO
INDOMITABLE CITY

Sacramento won federal funds for a new federal building at Seventh and K Streets that included a postal facility to handle the increasing volume of mail coming into the city (shown here in 1894).

THE
MAKING OF AMERICA
SERIES

SACRAMENTO
INDOMITABLE CITY

STEVEN M. AVELLA

ARCADIA

First printed 2003.
Reprinted 2004.

Published by Arcadia Publishing
an imprint of Tempus Publishing Inc.
Charleston SC, Chicago, Portsmouth NH, San Francisco

Printed in Great Britain

Library of Congress Catalog Card Number: 2003108859

For all general information contact Arcadia Publishing at:
Telephone 843-853-2070
Fax 843-853-0044
E-Mail sales@arcadiapublishing.com
For customer service and orders:
Toll-Free 1-888-313-2665

Visit us on the Internet at http://www.arcadiapublishing.com

Front cover: *Pedestrians cross the street at busy Eighth and K.*

CONTENTS

ACKNOWLEDGMENTS

I am deeply indebted to the authors whose works I have used in putting together this history of Sacramento. Their work is found on every page. Any error is my own. Special thanks go to James Henley, Joseph Pitti, Mead Kibbey, and William Mahan, who read the text and scanned it for errors of omission and commission. My dear, patient friend, Susan Silva, read the various drafts and took time off work to help me with picture selection. I am grateful to Ruth Ellis and her staff at the Sacramento Room at the City Library for their excellent resources and service. Likewise, Gary Kurutz and the staff of the California Room of the State Library have also provided a rich array of resources. A brief stint as an adjunct at California State University Sacramento allowed me to sample a variety of master's theses and student papers related to Sacramento topics. The staff at Arcadia Publishing, especially editors Jim Kempert, Rob Kangas, and Barbie Langston, have been marvelous. My deepest thanks go to James Henley, Pat Johnson, and the entire "family" of researchers, volunteers, and scholars that gather at the Sacramento Archives and Museum Collection Center (SAMCC). For years these archivists, curators, and historians have been my colleagues and friends as I have pursued any number of Sacramento themes. I could not begin to reciprocate all the favors they have done for me. To Jim Henley and the SAMCC staff and volunteers do I gratefully dedicate this book.

—Steven M. Avella

Associate Professor of History, Marquette University, Milwaukee, Wisconsin.

Photo credits: SAMCC (pp. 12, 13 courtesy California State Library Collection; p. 25 courtesy Edwin Beach Collection; p. 110 courtesy Antonia Castenada Collection; pp. 75, 102, 125 courtesy Frank Christy Collection; p. 136 courtesy Franz Dicks Collection; p. 105 courtesy Mather Field Collection; pp. 2, 8, 10, 14, 18, 19, 21, 22, 29, 30, 34, 37, 39, 40, 42, 43, 44, 46, 49, 52–54, 57, 59, 63, 64, 67, 70, 76, 79, 83, 84, 91, 147 courtesy Eleanor McClatchy Collection; p. 89 courtesy Arthur H. McCurdy Collection; back cover and pp. 33, 50, 69, 96, 98, 106, 109, 112, 115, 116, 118, 121, 123, 128, 135, 136, 138, 141, 144, 155 courtesy *Sacramento Bee* Collection; p. 151 courtesy Sacramento Chapter of the American Society of Civil Engineers Collection; pp. 131, 142, 145 courtesy Sacramento Ethnic Survey Collection; front cover and pp. 60, 92, 126 courtesy Sacramento Metropolitan Chamber of Commerce Collection; p. 27 courtesy Sacramento Society of California Pioneers Collection; p. 81 and p. 86 [Silver Wings Collection] courtesy Sacramento Valley Photography Survey Collection; pp. 149, 152 courtesy *Suttertown News* Collection; p. 134 Unknown Collection; p. 95 courtesy Joyce Vernon Collection; p. 73 courtesy Weinstock-Lubin Collection)

INTRODUCTION

Indomitable is an old-fashioned word. "Unconquered" and "not easily subdued" are terms usually applied to individuals, nations, or causes. But when city leaders in Sacramento crafted a new city seal in the early 1860s, they chose the classical Latin "Urbs Indomita"—Indomitable City—to characterize the California state capital. Indeed, the first years of Sacramento's existence did not bode well for the future. By the time the city seal was adopted, the city had already survived all-consuming fires, disastrous floods, and catastrophic epidemics. It had an unstable population, hot summers, and damp winters. Some believed that the site, picked largely for the convenience of gold miners who only needed a place to get off the boat, would fade into oblivion as did other gold rush towns. But something different happened here. By an act of its collective will, Sacramento decided to fight back. Instead of surrendering to the raging waters of the two rivers that embraced the city (the American and the Sacramento), they built levees. To combat the scourge of fire, they mandated brick construction for the commercial district. Sacramento even managed to snag the prize of the state capital, which had bounced around several Northern California towns. Sacramento's first miracle was that it survived the gold rush and its aftermath; other California communities didn't. One effusive publicist, writing boilerplate for a historical celebration commemorating the "Days of '49" in the 1920s, made this observation: "Columbia, Mokelumne Hill, Aurora . . . Seven Forks, Jackass Hill, Angel's Camp, Poker Flat—all famous in the days of old and the days of gold—live now for the most part in the memories of other and better times, while Sacramento fulfilled its destiny." To be a part of Sacramento was to participate in an ethic of survival and to continually seek new ways to adapt the city and its development to ever changing situations. Sacramento exists today because it was indomitable. No one easily subdued it.

The following pages provide a sweeping historical overview of the city of Sacramento, California. Home to native peoples like the Nisenan and Miwok, explored and examined by Spanish soldiers and padres, settled by an ambitious Swiss adventurer, Sacramento burst into urban life during one of America's periods of mass hysteria, the gold rush. Here, local merchants and entrepreneurs decided to open their shops along the banks of the Sacramento River and to survey and plat the lands running east and south of the two rivers.

Sacramento had the good fortune of being the western origin hub of the transcontinental railroad. Its ability to process and market the produce of California's rich Central Valley assured its economic viability. But if some believed the city's survival to be the working out of some inexorable "destiny" or the fulfillment of some unchangeable purpose, they couldn't be more wrong. For those who fought, planned, and executed the schemes and developments that kept the city alive, the city's future unfurled as the result of much courage, vision, and hard work, and also because of Sacramentans' conscious desire to keep the city vital no matter what the challenge. Indomitability is in Sacramento's collective DNA. Like all American cities, Sacramento is the product of purposeful human planning that at times cooperates with and, more often than not, overcomes the liabilities of its environment.

Today the city is at the center of a rapidly expanding metropolitan area and is the capital of a state with the fifth largest economy in the world. As yet, Sacramento's history has not been studied as thoroughly nor has the city received as much attention as its two coastal competitors, San Francisco and Los Angeles. But that is changing. Professional historians like Mark Eifler, Albert Hurtado, and Kenneth Owens have brought new perspectives to selected eras of the city's early years and to important figures like John Sutter. Sociologists and others note the ways in which the city has accommodated a remarkable diversity throughout its history as Sacramento has become a crossroads of sorts of the larger American reality. Journalists on the Lehrer News Hours, in search of a diverse American community, have interviewed Sacramentans as representative American citizens. Literary figures like Joan Didion and Richard Rodriguez reflect on their formative years in Sacramento and bring to it a new appreciation of ways in which it influenced their respective imaginations. To travel down its tree-lined streets, to sample life in its ever-renewing downtown, and to share the advantages of Sacramento's natural environment, its purposeful building of city institutions, and its distinct urban culture is to step into the living reality of the indomitable city.

The early seal for Sacramento City boasts the motto Urbs Indomita, *Indomitable City.*

1. PREHISTORY TO THE GOLD RUSH

Sacramento is the capital of the most populous state of the American Union. From its beginnings as one of many small gold rush era towns, it became a political, social, and economic hub of California's interior. Today it stands at the center of a five county metropolitan area that embraces over a million inhabitants and continues to grow.

THE PHYSICAL ENVIRONMENT

Sacramento is located in the "other California," the vast Central Valley that runs 450 miles through the heart of the Golden State. The valley was once part of the ocean floor, and in its prehistoric period, four great mountain ranges emerged—the Sierra Nevada to the east, the Klamath and the Cascades to the north, and the Coastal Range to the west. These mountains surrounded a huge depression into which they poured waters, sand, gravel, and other sediment. Eventually this "inland sea" receded, some say by bursting through the Coastal Range at Carquinez, leaving behind a valley containing volcanic rock and alluvial fans, the latter from the washed rock of the Coastal Range. But the valley's key characteristic is its flatness.

Sacramento is located in the northern part of this valley, an area watered by the Sacramento River. The Sacramento Valley represents a distinct region of the larger Central Valley. As historian Joseph McGowan has noted, "The physical geography of the valley has been a continuous factor in valley history. Transportation, settlement, irrigation, reclamation, floods and agriculture have all reflected this physical environment, especially the presence of the rivers." The Sacramento River begins on the southern slopes of the Klamath and provides the central waterway for the valley. Into it flow tributary streams fed from snow-capped mountains to the east. To the south, the waters of the Cosumnes and American Rivers also run into the Sacramento. Dozens of smaller streams with names like Antelope, Deer, Mill, and Butte enter the Sacramento as well. Three creeks—Stony Creek, Cache Creek and Putah Creek—add to the river's flow.

These waterways bring a rich diversity of soils and dump them on the ground in alluvial fans, providing the basis for the rich agriculture of the valley, an important ingredient in Sacramento's economic stability.

Like many American cities, Sacramento's destiny was shaped by its strategic location. Situated on low lands at the confluence of the Sacramento and American Rivers, Sacramento was initially a gateway for the legendary Argonauts of '49, a convenient drop-off point for miners and a place where they returned for supplies and recreation. Later, the agricultural riches of the valley were "mined" and processed by enterprising Sacramentans. Venture capitalists underwrote these endeavors and evolving transportation systems conveyed them to markets all over the nation and the world.

Sacramento stands out, as one popular history called it, a "City of the Plain." Although the valley slopes steadily from Red Bluff to Sacramento, the perception of the land around Sacramento is flatness. Indeed, visitors seeing its skyline today from the east or west can see the stark lines of its nest of tall buildings from a great distance. The city can be oppressively hot during summer but, thanks to the oceanic breezes that come up through the Sacramento Delta, often pleasantly cool enough in the evenings. Winters are often damp and rainy with daytime temperatures hovering in the 50s and 60s, while nights sometime plunge to the 40s and 30s. Snow and freezing rain are unusual, but on rare occasions Sacramento has been blanketed in winter white. Precipitation varies from year to

Albert Bierstadt portrays a romantic, pastoral Sacramento Valley.

year. Some years, the rains barely soak the soil. Other years, the heavens open in such a deluge that fear of flooding is real.

Archaeologist Norman Wilson relates that the valley was inhabited by ancient prehistoric creatures: mastodons, horses, camels, ferocious saber-toothed tigers, huge bears, and fearless wolves. Flocks of waterfowl clouded the skies. Fish like sturgeon and salmon were found in abundance while large herds of elk, deer, and antelope roamed at will. California's symbolic grizzly also gamboled through the region. Giant oaks, sycamores, cottonwoods, willows, and ash once dominated the land near Sacramento's rivers, creeks, and streams. Wild oats grew in abundance, tules choked the riverbanks, and open patches of heavy grass flourished in flat areas. Human settlement, however, permanently altered the environment. Trees were cut down, wetlands filled in, and ecosystems that once sustained prehistoric life were disrupted. The mountains surrounding the valley meant that it was isolated from the rest of the world. Indeed, because it was so remote, population grew slowly in Sacramento and in California's interior in general for many years.

HUMAN DEVELOPMENT IN PREHISTORIC SACRAMENTO

The lure of the valley was its abundant natural resources. No one is quite sure if the first inhabitants came from the north and east, working their way down the coast, or came up from the south, but no doubt they were nomadic food-gatherers who discovered a rich treasure trove in the valley. The first humans arrived more than 12,000 years ago. The simple law of inertia may have contributed to the first settlements in the valley; people simply found everything they needed and did not want to scale any of the mountain chains to get out.

Permanent villages appeared as people hunted and adapted their food-gathering techniques to accommodate their locality. Native peoples became skilled anglers and hunters. They discovered in the seeds and nuts of the area a new and nutritious food source. Indeed, the millions of acorns that fell from the abundant oaks provided an important and preservable staple for Indian peoples who settled in the area.

The Indians of the Central Valley were a varied and variegated lot with different languages, cultures, and ways of life. Early images of them were largely derived from the observations of white explorers like Jedediah Smith, who characterized the Sacramento Nisenan as "degraded" and "miserable." Later, literary figures such as Gertrude Atherton described the tribes as "lethargic." Hinton R. Helper, a notorious apologist for southern slavery, also weighed in with negative observations on California natives, characterizing them as "filthy and abominable." The offensive ethnocentricity of these comments stand in sharp contrast to the recent scholarship of archaeologists, historians, and ethnographers who have evaluated these tribal peoples on their own terms and provided a new framework for understanding them. The Native Americans skillfully adapted to their environment. Among the tribes of California existed a diversity of languages, housing and clothing styles, religions, and life-passage customs. In Sacramento

An Indian woman whose clothing reflects European influence grinds acorns and seeds.

County, the two major Indian groups that dominated the region were the Nisenan and Miwok. Both of these spoke a variety of the Penutian phylum of languages (other tribes that shared them were the Coastanoan, Wintun, and Yokuts).

The Nisenan, the group that occupied most of the area later encompassed by the city of Sacramento, was a branch of the Maidu (sometimes referred to as the Southern Maidu). This group occupied strategic areas along the rivers. One tribal center at the mouth of the American River was called Pusune. Villages between the Cosumnes River and the south fork of the American River, near Placerville, formed another important center. East along the American River were the villages of Sek and Kadema. Between the mouth of the American River and Folsom there were estimated to be ten village sites—four of them in present-day Sacramento alone: Momel at present-day Fifth and Richards, Samor at Fifth and J, Yalis at 30th and B, and another at today's city plaza. Unfortunately, native names were ignored by European settlers, thereby erasing memory of their presence in the area for many years.

Isolation was a defining feature of Nisenan life. Historians suggest that they had few contacts outside their tribelet. They existed in an uneasy relationship with other tribal groups in the area, particularly the Plains-Miwok who lived south of the Cosumnes River. Nisenan people lived in a variety of settings. Some existed in small, extended family groupings of 15–25 people. Others lived in fairly large villages numbering over 500. The central village often acted as the pole of a more extended settlement pattern, and the headman of the village drew these tributary villages together for religious and social gatherings and for hunting. Valley Nisenan lived in dome-shaped houses 10–15 feet across made from cut saplings placed in holes at the perimeter and bent inward toward the center. These were covered with earth, tules, and grasses around an excavated hole in the earth that sank the structure anywhere from 12 to 24 inches. In larger villages, tribes had a similar but larger semi-subterranean structure called a "kum" or dance house with a smoke hole in the center. Sweat houses (one was on present-day J Street) and acorn granaries were also common in village life. As with every tribelet, Nisenan peoples laid out cemeteries, trading sites, ceremonial grounds, and sacred spaces for shrines.

Nisenan people were food-gatherers, taking advantage of the abundance around them. Hunting, gathering, and fishing went on year-round, but in the late summer and early fall, extended families and villages gathered the precious acorn. Drained of its bitter tannic acid, the acorn provided sustenance in times of food scarcity as it was eaten as mush or bread. Nisenan, however, were omniverous. Deer drives were a common collective endeavor, while black bears, wild cats, mountain lions, and rabbits provided pelts and occasionally food. Nisenan people ate birds and fish of various kinds and also insects such as grasshoppers that they drove out of the bushes and roasted. To the horror of visiting Europeans, Nisenan people often wore few clothes (a trait adopted by later inhabitants of Sacramento,

An Indian spears salmon.

especially during the torrid summer months). Men often went naked or wore only a breech cloth. Women were bare breasted, wearing only short skirts made of local materials.

Social structure among the Nisenan focused on the headman, a chief or captain who received his authority from the leaders of each extended family and from the village shamans. The headman arbitrated disputes, convened the people to discuss major problems, and oversaw the gathering activities. Property was both communal and personal. Families staked out fishing sites and oak groves while each person kept his or her own personal hunting accouterments. Women owned and could inherit cooking utensils.

The Nisenan found the meaning of their world through religious symbols and myths. Mountains like Mount Diablo and the Sutter Buttes were invested with religious significance. Like every society, the Nisenan had myths to explain the reasons for existence and the purpose of life. Creation stories include the activity of a trinity of beings: a huge turtle that brought the earth up from the bottom of the sea, a world creator who fashioned the land, and the coyote, a human spirit who did both good and bad in bringing about the human race. Religious expression took form in various cultic rituals. The most elaborate form of Nisenan ritual, the Kuksu ceremony, consisted of a dance, done by initiates with costumed feather headbands who represented the spirits of gods. The ceremonies were held in winter inside a large, earth-covered dance house. Another religious observance ritualized mourning with an annual celebration in late September or early October. This involved a ritual marking of days and the construction of a central pyre around which mourners and dancers performed as the belongings of

Nisenan villages consisted of semi-subterranean, dome-shaped houses.

the deceased were burned. Rituals indicating the change of seasons included the Kamin Dance, which celebrated the beginning of spring, and the Lole Dance honoring the first fruit. The Nisenan had doctors or shamans, whose ceremonies also took place in the dance house. The religious doctor or *ocpe* gained control over spirits through dreams or other specialized experiences. He was the chief bridge between the human and the supernatural and figured prominently in the rituals of the dance.

While the Nisenan were the primary people living on the lands later to be encompassed by Sacramento, nearby were the Miwok, another Penutian-speaking people with a different culture. Miwoks did concentrate south of the Cosumnes River, but through intermarriage and sometimes-permeable boundaries, they also figured into the ethnographic realities of the region. The Valley Miwok (one of three groups including the Coast and Lake Miwok) were also food-gatherers like the nearby Nisenan, subsisting on acorns, small game, and fish. One distinction of Miwok culture was that some of its tribal members had actually been sent to the missions and inducted into the religio-cultural world of the Spanish settlers. These interior converts—called *tularenos* by the mission padres because they lived in the tule-choked areas along the rivers—were to be a beachhead for subsequent missionization of the California interior. Miwok people in general, however, were resistant to Spanish influence.

CONTACT AND ENCOUNTER WITH EUROPEAN CULTURE

The eighteenth century, a great epoch of European contact with California, brought some of the first Europeans to the Central Valley. The Spanish were the first to explore the valley as part of their larger policy of extending influence and settlement into Alta California. From the beachhead of presidios, pueblos, and missions along the coast, forays into the Central Valley took place. However, the valley held no particular allure and early encounters were from a distance. Spanish explorer (and later governor) Pedro Fages recorded his vista of the Sacramento Valley in 1772 as he looked over the broad area from a spur of Mount Diablo around present-day Antioch. On this same expedition, Franciscan Friar Juan Crespi looked out over the Sacramento Delta and beheld a land "as level as the palm of the hand." In 1776, Juan Bautista de Anza headed an expedition that slightly probed into the delta.

In the nineteenth century, the pace of exploration and engagement picked up. In September 1808, Ensign Gabriel Moraga left with 13 soldiers from Mission San Jose to explore the rivers, locate Indian settlements, and scout for possible mission sites. He was also charged (an order he wisely ignored) with recapturing *tularenos* who had abandoned the missions. He reached the American River between present-day Rancho Cordova and Folsom in October, calling the American *Las Llagas* (literally "the wounds" to commemorate the suffering of Christ). His most significant move, in terms of the future state capital of California, was his naming of the Feather River, the Rio del Santissimo

15

Sacramento—the River of the Most Blessed Sacrament (a reference to the Catholic doctrine of the real presence of Christ in the Eucharist). He then moved west to the present Sacramento River and named it the Jesus Maria. He followed the east bank of the river upstream as far north as Butte City before he turned back. Moraga had mixed encounters with the Indians and reported negatively to his superiors on the possibility of a mission in the Central Valley. His advice would be followed.

However, others still believed that California's mission chain should extend into the Central Valley. A visit up the Sacramento River in October 1811, spearheaded by two Franciscan priests, Ramon Abella and Buenaventura Fortuini, suggested again that a Catholic outpost was needed in the area. Still, the Spanish were reluctant. In 1817, Abella returned with Friar Narciso Duran and Captain Luis Arguello, still looking for a good mission site. However, by this time Spain's grip on its American colonies was weakening. In 1821, Mexico declared its independence and California became a Mexican province.

European penetration continued. In 1823, a vessel of the Russian Imperial Navy led by Estonian Otto von Kotzebue is thought to have ascended the Sacramento as far as the American River. In this party were 20 Aleuts who camped near present-day Freeport. The American presence began in 1827 when the famous Jedediah "Bible Totin' " Smith explored the valley from the south and camped along the American River near the present-day site of California State University, Sacramento. Traveling east over the snowy Sierras, Smith related to his trapper friends and to others in the East the abundant resources in the region. The Hudson Bay Company headquartered at Fort Vancouver on the Columbia River took note of Smith's descriptions. Members of the Hudson Bay Company's fur brigades began to visit the valley every year from 1830 to 1844. Michel Laframboise was perhaps the best known of the Hudson Bay Company trappers. Other explorers noted the large size of the various Indian encampments they encountered. By the middle of the 1830s, as McGowan notes, the Sacramento Valley was increasingly well known, but visited only by transients looking for pelts. In May 1833, Captain Juan Bautista (John) Cooper, an American who became a naturalized Mexican citizen, petitioned for a land grant along the American River south of present-day Power Inn Road and Fruitridge. Cooper, however, never followed through on the application and allowed the petition to lapse.

Conflict with Native Americans was inevitable as more whites came into the region. Moraga was hit with flying debris during his trip in 1817. Armed clashes between trappers and Indians took place near the Cosumnes River near Galt in 1828. Some fighting was spurred by the growing practice of horse-stealing by the Miwok and other valley Indians. (Native peoples either ate or mounted the horses to improve their chances against Europeans.) But more fatal than lead or steel, the European encounter with the Indians of the Sacramento region brought deadly disease. In 1833, tribes' numbers were decimated by a devastating epidemic of malaria, brought by Hudson Bay Company trappers. This disease obliterated whole villages of the Nisenan and forced survivors into the hills. One estimate suggests that nearly 75 percent of the native population died during this plague. Those who survived were too weakened to resist white settlement. Scholars disagree over the number of Native Americans who lived in the Central Valley before and after the malaria epidemic. It is not known how many lived in the region of Sacramento. By 1839, however, the year John Augustus Sutter appeared to claim the lands that would make up the future city, the numbers were smaller than they had been before.

JOHN SUTTER AND HIS LEGACY

Sutter was the first European to establish a permanent settlement on the lands that would encompass the city. Different viewpoints exist on whether to accord the title "Founder of Sacramento" to John Sutter. Indeed, the first efforts at city-building in the region, the ill-fated town of Sutterville, were done at his direction. His role as a civic official was evidenced by his participation as judge for the election for magistrate of the Sacramento District in September 1846. But others note that the present city of Sacramento was born after he had sold the fort and repaired to his farm along the Yuba River. Like every other figure in the American West, Sutter has been the subject of revisionist scholarship. These scholars have noted that his life has been more defined by myth (some of it of his own making) than hard historical fact. Throughout most of Sacramento's history, he has been memorialized by a myriad of romantic accounts reprinted in tour guides, promotional materials, and even a host of books. He has even been the subject of a Hollywood movie. Even more, school children of the region were taught over the years to hail him as the founder of the state capital. Distilling the factual from the fanciful reveals a core of important facts about Sutter.

Johann Augustus Sutter was born February 15, 1803 in Kandern in the German margrave of Baden, 13 miles north of Basel, Switzerland. He was the son of Johann Jakob Sutter, a foreman in the paper mill, and Christina Wilhelmina Strober, a clergyman's daughter from Grenzach, located up the Rhine River. Sutter grew up in Kandern, a town that witnessed the movements of Napoleon's army, and one historian suggests that Sutter's love for the military, for uniforms and military pomp stemmed from his boyhood experiences of witnessing armies coming and going through his native town. He left Kandern at age 15 and attended school at Neuchatel, Switzerland, and he began an apprenticeship with Emmanuel Thurneysen, a publisher, bookseller, and printer in Basel. Sutter did not take to the publishing and bookselling trade and quit Basel for a job as a draper's clerk in nearby Aarburg. There he met Anna or Annette Dubeld and impregnated her, marrying her one day before the birth of his first child, a son they named Johann Augustus Sutter, Jr. Four more children followed. Sutter had by then moved to the Canton of Bern, where Annette's mother, a comfortable widow in Burgdorf, financed him in a dry goods business. When this failed, he entered the reserve corps at Bern in 1828, rising to the rank of first under-lieutenant. In later years he embellished this

Adventurer and settler John (Johann) Augustus Sutter embellished his brief military career and fostered a boyhood love for military titles and regalia.

slim military record with stories of participation in campaigns in Spain in 1823–1824 and service under the French King Charles X at Grenoble in 1830. Sutter never lost his boyhood love of military titles and regalia. For whomever he worked, Mexican or American governments, he always managed to wangle titles such as "Captain" or "General."

Sutter's love for titles and his own exaggerated accounts of his past life contributed to the historic romanticization of him by successive generations of Sacramentans. However, modern historians are not so slow to ignore his short-comings and quick to pierce the bubble of his sometimes egregious self-promotion. Among his many character defects, Sutter had an unfortunate propensity to pile up debts and compounded his problems by continuing to borrow. This provided the context for his hasty departure from Europe. In mid-May 1834, he secretly liquidated his assets and abandoned his struggling family, taking passage for America and landing in New York. He not only left behind his family but also a host of debts.

Sutter became a trader and set out for Missouri, the gateway to the American West, with two German and two French companions. He arrived first in St. Louis where he met a Westphalian, Johann August Laufkotter, with whom he traveled for two years. Here, his biographers note, Sutter began to embellish his previous life (free from worry that anyone would check the veracity of his stories). In Missouri, Sutter witnessed the adventure and profit potential in the commercial exploitation of the American West. In 1835 and 1836, Sutter joined two caravans headed for the lucrative trading center of Santa Fe. On the way he learned the importance of Bent's Fort, a military/commercial outpost on the upper Arkansas River in present-day Colorado that functioned as a magnet for commercial interaction between whites and Indians. Some have suggested that this was the model for Sutter's Fort in Sacramento. (Others claim it was Fort Vancouver or Sitka.) Through a fellow traveler on the Santa Fe expedition, fur-trader Charles Beaubien, he also heard stories of far-off California with its natural wealth and soft climate.

At Santa Fe, Sutter's less than honest side emerged when he became involved in a scheme that defrauded some of his German clients. His companion Laufkotter soon came to mistrust his voluble and glad-handing friend. When the situation became untenable in 1837, Sutter simply moved further west and spent a year in Westport, Missouri (today Kansas City). Here too, in pursuit of commercial success, Sutter skirted the boundaries of the law and of propriety by selling illegal whiskey and enjoying sexual favors from Shawnee women.

A year later, when his presence in Westport became compromised, Sutter gathered a small band (including a young Indian boy he had "purchased"), linked up with a group representing the American Fur Company, and accompanied them west along the Oregon Trail, reaching western Oregon in early November. He tarried for a time in the Willamette Valley and then moved north to the headquarters of the Hudson Bay Company at Fort Vancouver. Here he was anxious to head directly south to California, but officials of the company dissuaded him from the winter-time trek and urged instead that he go first to

Prior to the discovery of gold, Sutter's Fort was the first stop for settlers coming into what would become Sacramento.

Hawaii. Sutter concurred and with eight companions boarded the *Columbia*, making for Honolulu in mid-December. In the Hawaiian kingdom, he claimed that he had so impressed King Kameahamea III that the monarch wanted him to stay and command his native army. But Sutter was restless to move on, so the Polynesian king let him go with the gift of ten indentured servants—two women and eight men for three years. These *kanakas* as they became known were invaluable to Sutter in his projects.

Sutter left Hawaii and visited the Russian colony at New Archangel (Sitka), Alaska. Here he learned of yet another commercial opportunity as he heard of the fur trade—pelts claimed from sea otters and seals—and of the Russian commercial outpost near Bodega Bay, Fort Ross. He then set sail on the brig *Clementine* for Mexican California and on July 4, 1839 was deposited in Monterey, the capital of the province. He arrived at a time when the Mexican government was concerned about the frequency of American incursions into the Central Valley. Of the valley Sutter had no doubt learned much from the Hudson Bay officials at Fort Vancouver and the Russians at Sitka—both of whom had given him coveted letters of recommendation to Alta California Governor Juan Bautista Alvarado. He presented himself to Alvarado and requested the opportunity to establish a rancho in the valley. The Mexican governor surely believed that the eager stranger could serve his goal of pacifying and securing California's interior and also curtail the activities of Indians who used inland bases to stage horse-stealing raids on coastal ranches. He freely gave Sutter permission to pick a site, settle on it, and then return a year hence to file for Mexican citizenship and apply for the land grant he desired.

Before he debarked, Sutter consulted with the Russians at Fort Ross. He also stopped to visit with General Mariano Vallejo at Sonoma. Sutter then proceeded up the Sacramento River on a small schooner, the *Isabella,* along with a smaller boat, both of which he had chartered in Yerba Buena (San Francisco). His crew contained a medley of nationalities, both German carpenters and *kanakas*. Using Miwok guides (who deftly directed him away from their territories), Sutter meandered along the riverbanks until he finally traveled upstream on the American River. Near the Nisenan Pusune Rancheria, a short distance from the mouth of the river, he unloaded his vessel and pitched his tents. The local Indians may have feared that Sutter was hunting for escaped mission Indians, but he made gestures of friendship and conciliation. Nonetheless, Sutter still felt compelled to remind the native inhabitants of the deadly firepower of Europeans. Shortly after his landing, he symbolically positioned the three cannons he had brought with him from Hawaii and fired a nine-gun salute when the *Isabella* (with several who bailed out of the project) sailed back to San Francisco. The roar of the guns frightened elk and deer and put thousands of waterfowl to flight, and it reminded the native inhabitants that Sutter meant to defend himself.

The *kanakas* made temporary grass huts near the river. Sutter moved a bit south of the landing to higher ground and there began his fort, which grew slowly but surely on a small knoll well back from the rivers.

Sutter's land grant was redrawn by Jean Jacques Vioget, who made the original in 1841.

CREATING THE NEW OUTPOST

On August 29, 1840, Sutter petitioned Governor Alvarado for Mexican citizenship and then made application for his land grant. This claim would later become the subject of a great deal of controversy. During the winter of 1840–1841, Sutter engaged engineer and navigator Jean Jacques Vioget, a former Swiss drummer in Napoleon's army, to make a survey and prepare the maps required by the Mexican officials to validate his land grant. Sutter believed that his grant lay between the present Sutterville Road and a line drawn east to west through the northern edge of the Sutter Buttes and from the Sacramento River to a line a few miles east of the Feather River. However, Vioget, who used homemade equipment to plot the location, made an error of 14 miles on the southern boundary, drawing a latitude 11-and-a-half miles north of the American River. Ironically, not even Sutter's Fort was included in the map, and since the grant specified that Sutter was not to include in his possessions the overflow lands of the river, the site of modern Sacramento was also excluded. The ensuing confusion of land titles was further complicated when the two copies of Vioget's map were lost. McGowan notes that although there would be controversy, the basic outline of Sutter's grant included lands along the south bank of the American

This has been called the "earliest known" painting of Sutter's Fort.

River from the big bend near Brighton (present site of California State University at Sacramento) to the fort, the area around Sutterville, and both banks of the Feather River from a point west of present-day Nicolaus to a few miles north of Marysville. Sutter's grant was not an unbroken area, but rather a few choice regions along the river where the soil was deep and the site accessible by water.

In 1841, Sutter was awarded 11 leagues or 44,000 acres of an "empresario" grant that envisioned a colony of Swiss families. Thus, he named the territory Nueva Helvetia (New Switzerland). The main requirement of an empresario grant was that the grantee had to settle 12 families on the land. Sutter began to organize the area according to his plans to establish an inland empire. Using the clay-like soils found around the area, Indian laborers constructed modest adobe buildings and finally a rectangular fortress measuring 300 by 160 feet with high walls. Bastions crowned the northwest and southwest corners. Within the fort, Sutter constructed buildings to be used for residences and shops. New Helvetia was from the start intended to make money for Sutter and to establish him as a benign grandee of the area. This first outpost of European civilization was and continues to be historically significant. The fort, allowed to fall into ruins after Sutter quit the area in 1850, was nearly totally destroyed until the romantic 1890s when the Native Sons of the Golden West began its restoration, a project that the State of California finished. The fort is today one of Sacramento's most important tourist attractions.

From the fort, commercial and development activities were launched. Imitating what he had seen of Anglo-American, British, and Russian traders, Franciscan missionaries, and Californios, Sutter made his profits through Indian labor. Sutter's relationships with the Indians were often rocky, and despite their growing dependence on white goods, the Nisenans actually kept their distance from Sutter. Eventually, however, a combination of bribes and force drew them into his service. He learned the social system of the Nisenan and Miwoks and appealed to the local headmen for help in securing workers. Soon a respectable Indian workforce, watched over by white overseers, was in place. During the all-important wheat harvest, close to 600 Indians worked in Sutter's fields. Sutter's wealth, as Albert Hurtado notes, was built almost totally on Indian labor.

Indeed, their hard work was the economic lifeline of the fort. They hunted for pelts and game; they processed animal hides and rendered precious tallow for candles. They made the adobe bricks that were used for the fort, they planted and harvested the grain crops, and they tended herds of cattle, sheep, and pigs. Sutter even drafted the Indians into a makeshift army (replete with uniforms purchased from the departing Russians at Fort Ross). With these "troops" he warded off Miwok raids on his fields and herds and launched a punitive expedition against the Mokelumne Miwok, who were stealing horses and selling them to traders. Nonetheless, Indians were not passive recipients of Sutter's direction. Some rebelled and fled his service. Sutter employed corporal punishment to keep Indians in line and violently punished two "rebellious" Miwoks, Rufino and Raphero, placing the head of Raphero on a grisly pike outside the fort. Sutter also used Indian labor to pay off debts he owed to creditors like Antonio Sunol and William Leidesdorff.

Acts of violence notwithstanding, Sutter's conquest of the Indians came primarily through his attaching them to a European system of peonage and commerce. He also sold them liquor. Indians were paid in European goods that they craved. Sutter issued metal disks to the Indians that were punched with a distinctive hole for a day's labor. These disks, worn like a necklace, were redeemable only in Sutter's store, increasing their growing dependence on white accouterments. Two weeks' work, for example, secured a muslin shirt or cotton for trousers. Most Indians who worked for Sutter were not slaves but peonized labor, as was true throughout the Mexican empire. In this first set of economic activities, the city's modern commercial life was born.

Sutter also altered the patterns of native life by injecting new work demands into the traditional cycle of food-gathering that had marked the life of the Central Valley tribes. The Native Americans learned to adapt to European work schedules and notions of time. He altered traditional Miwok and Nisenan marriage customs such as polygamy, forbidding chiefs from having more than one or two wives. To prevent the domination of women by the chiefs, Sutter matched eligible Indian women with available males. Sutter himself, however, continued to cohabit with a number of women. Before his abandoned wife, Annette Dubeld, caught up with him in 1850, Sutter lived with a *kanaka* woman named Manuiki and also consorted with Indian women, according to the negative recollections of one of his overseers, Heinrich Lienhard.

Sutter's Fort was also a workshop, providing small manufactured goods and supplies for those coming into the province and anxious to settle in California.

Sutter himself served as a generous grandee for those who subsequently received large grants to other parts of the valley. The New Helvetia grant was but the first viable land concession made by the Mexican government in the Sacramento Valley, and imposed a new arrangement of property holding, development, and future historical development on the northern valley. Sutter's Fort was also the first stop for other grantees in what would become Sacramento County. John Sinclair and his wife, Mary, were the first settlers on the Del Paso land grant, north of the American River, one of the last to be broken up. To the east of Del Paso were Rancho San Juan and Rancho Rio de los Americanos. To the south of New Helvetia, the Mexican government awarded the Omochumnes or Sheldon grant to Jared Sheldon. Peter Lassen and William Ide received land from Mexico farther north in the valley. Sutter helped Pierson B. Reading receive lands from Mexico. John Bidwell, an overland immigrant who was a major player in the founding of the city of Chico and one of Sutter's first faithful retainers, arrived with the Bidwell-Bartelson party in 1841 and worked alongside his patron, taking over his Hock Farm operation in 1844. Bidwell did not receive lands from Mexico but from a former landholder near Chico.

THE DYNAMIC OF MANIFEST DESTINY

Ultimately, Sutter's New Helvetia was drawn into the vortex of larger events taking place within the Mexican empire and in the rapidly expanding United States. In 1844, Sutter became enmeshed in a complicated internal struggle for dominance in California that pitted Governor Manuel Micheltorena against a cabal led by General Jose Castro. Loyal to Micheltorena, Sutter assembled a military force and marched south to fight the governor's foes. A series of shifting alliances left Sutter out on a limb, and he was captured at the Battle of Cahuenga. Micheltorena was deposed, but his successor Pio Pico and his allies did not punish the Sacramento adventurer. However, when he returned to his fort in 1845, he found things unraveling. Many of his native workers had fled, and Sutter responded with violence, executing the Miwok Raphero. Continual difficulties with the Native Americans ensued.

Even more importantly, in the 1840s, a burst of ideologically inspired expansionism gripped the popular imagination. Manifest Destiny, as it was termed, summoned American economic and cultural energies to press the new nation westward to the Pacific Coast. Thousands upon thousands began the trek west, hoping to find land, security, and fortune in what Anglos perceived was an "undeveloped wilderness." Sutter soon began to catch the wave of westward migrants, and his fort became an important stopping-off point for visitors who continued to make their way into the valley. Hunters, trappers, and British sailors (who had deserted in San Francisco) were welcomed at the fort—all receiving warm and gracious hospitality from Sutter, whose reputation as a generous and congenial host left many warm memories, even among his critics. The overland emigrants, tired and worn out from the strenuous journey and in particular the arduous trek over the Sierras, found Sutter's Fort an oasis. In 1844, the Townsend-Stevens-Murphy Party brought wagons over the top of the Sierras. Two years later, the ill-fated Donner Party unsuccessfully tried to do the same. It was Sutter who attempted to bring succor to the trapped and starving party by donating flour, meat, and some horses.

U.S. interest in California began to peak as well, especially with the expansionist politics of the Democratic Party in the 1840s. By 1841, the mapping expedition of Captain Charles Wilkes had sent a group of scientists to Sutter's Fort to examine the territory. One of the West's most intrepid explorers, John Charles Fremont, then a lieutenant in the U.S. Corps of Topographical Engineers, crossed the Sierra in the winter of 1844 in company with scout Kit Carson. Coming down to Sacramento, he encouraged Anglo settlers in the valley to rise up against Mexico. He too was graciously received by Sutter, who fed and supplied him. This growing American presence presaged the disruption of relations with Mexico that began to intensify after the election of expansionist James Knox Polk in 1844. By mid-1846, the United States and Mexico were at war. A local revolutionary movement, begun in Sacramento County, raised the standard of revolt and hoisted up the Bear Flag as a symbol of secession from Mexico. With the onset of hostilities, Colonel Fremont captured Sutter's Fort and temporarily renamed it "Fort Sacramento." An incurable opportunist, Sutter acquiesced in the American take-over and even accepted an appointment as a U.S. Federal Indian Subagent in 1847. He even permitted, after months of negotiation, the interment of General Mariano Vallejo at the fort. By 1848, the Treaty of Guadalupe Hidalgo ended the war and allowed the purchase of California by the United States.

Explorer John Charles Fremont encouraged Anglo settlers to rise up against Mexico.

While Sutter managed to tailor his loyalties appropriately during these days of transition, the dynamics of change affected his dreams for New Helvetia. The shifting politics and the disruptions of his labor supply placed his plans for an inland empire in jeopardy. Sutter owed money to virtually everyone. He gradually realized that he had to market the lands of his grant.

CITY BUILDING

Interestingly, few of the many immigrants who availed themselves of Sutter's legendary hospitality remained in the area, in part because Sutter himself seemed disinclined to create a city or a town around his fort that could sustain a stable population. However, by 1845, this changed, and Sutter began to plan a city along the river. His first effort at city building took place on a plot of land 3 miles downstream on the Sacramento River, a location with banks high enough to keep back the waters that occasionally flooded the areas around the fort. "Tomorrow we are surveying at least the town or city: but not close by the fort," Sutter wrote to Pierson B. Reading on January 29, 1845. His friend John Bidwell surveyed the site working together with pioneer immigrant Lansford B. Hastings. The new city was near the intersection of present-day Sutterville Road and the Sacramento River. The grid planned by the surveyor contained 200 lots. Later the town was named "Suttersville" and finally "Sutterville." However, as with many of Sutter's moneymaking schemes, he soon lost control of the project to his creditors. Hastings managed to gain title to many of the lots, along with Bidwell and another early Sacramentan, George McKinstry. Sutterville might have proven a more popular site than Sacramento, but a number of events intervened that shifted the foundation of the city to the north along the riverfront.

Debt had stalked Sutter throughout his life and, lacking a benefactor or a company or a royal patron, he had been compelled to finance the fort himself. In the end, the money he borrowed and promised to repay eventually cut off his expansionist dreams. One of his more pressing notes was for $30,000, which he owed the Russians for the purchase of the contents of Fort Ross in 1841. Sutter had dismantled the building, the fort walls, and some of the redwood planking and moved it to New Helvetia. He also had acquired a schooner that he renamed the *Sacramento* and additional livestock, including 2,000 head of cattle, horses, and sheep driven overland to Sutter's Fort. The beginnings of American rule over California were the beginning of the end for Sutter and New Helvetia. Pressed by the debts he owed to so many, Sutter characteristically began to expand his operations.

With the help of a detachment of Mormons, who had arrived after the Mexican War, Sutter began to build a gristmill on the American River. Mormon leader Samuel Brannan also arrived at the fort, recognized the location as a good spot for retailing, and built a store outside the fort. In 1845, James Wilson Marshall arrived from Oregon. Hoping once again to provide needed commodities for the steady flow of people coming into the Central Valley, Sutter negotiated a treaty with the Koloma Indians to build a lumber sawmill on the banks of the American River.

With Marshall's skills as craftsman and mechanic, Sutter put him to work in the Sierras, near Coloma, to build the lumber mill, unwittingly setting in motion a new epoch of western and even world history when Marshall's workers discovered gold in the traces of the mill.

Sacramento had not yet been born in 1848, but some of its elements were already in place. Sutter had built a network of commercial activity that drew its wealth from the rich natural environment. Other settlers began to manufacture things that people needed: hides, tallow, food, and grain. Wealth was generated by the labor of the native peoples. The location was enhanced by its proximity to rivers and waterways, which could become vehicles of commerce. When gold was discovered, the world was turned upside down. By this time, however, Sutter had done as much as he could. The task of city formation and the creation of a community would be left to his son.

This 1848 view of the Sacramento landing, painted by C.A. Tabor, shows the foot of I Street. The vessel moored by the shanty is the Provinence, *which was dismantled and reconfigured into a store owned by George McDougal and William Blackburn.*

27

2. Gold, Nature, and City Building

The past was prelude in the formation of Sacramento. Indian inhabitants shaped the human ecology. Sutter and the people he attracted produced commercial possibilities, but it was the gold rush that created Sacramento. This massive movement of people and capital literally brought the world to the shores of the Sacramento River and created a center for social, commercial, and cultural exchange that exists to this day.

The Gold Mining Boom

Sacramento did not just happen; it was planned. Like so many cities in America, a handful of enterprising and even avaricious developers saw advantages to developing the site and took financial risks to do so. In Sacramento, this drive is embodied in the career of Samuel Brannan, who played a major role in the development of the city. Brannan was a native of Maine. Fleeing an abusive father, he made a picaresque journey across America, causing historian Kevin Starr to compare him to Mark Twain's Huck Finn. Brannan early on became interested in land speculation and lost money in his first efforts. To recoup his fortunes, he learned printing and became a writer and an editor. In the 1830s, he converted to Mormonism and turned his energies to the propagation of this expansive "westering" denomination, which was in its formative years. When the persecuted Mormons searched for a secluded site on which to construct their new Zion, Brannan laid his skills for writing and publishing at the service of the growing church. He combined his religious zeal with the expansionist doctrines of the Democratic Party of the 1840s and played a role in a scheme to settle Mormons in the Mexican province of California and then turn over their land to the U.S. government. These plans coincided with President James K. Polk's efforts to provoke war with Mexico in order to seize Texas and California. In February 1846, Brannan and a party of more than 200 left New York and arrived in Yerba Buena in July. By the time he arrived, the Mexican War had begun and California would soon be permanently detached from Mexico. Nonetheless, Brannan set to work to develop a Mormon enclave in California and also to create a profitable climate for land speculators. He and his followers built homes, shops, and food processing facilities. Brannan also began a newspaper, the *California Star*. As his new enterprise boomed, Brannan traveled back to Salt Lake in order to convince Brigham Young to relocate Mormon headquarters to California. Young balked and Brannan moved back west.

In 1847, Brannan formed a new partnership with fellow merchant C.C. Smith and opened a store at Sutter's Fort. Brannan had long seen the agriculture of the valley as an important component of future growth and wealth. His store traded groceries and other dry goods for raw grains, animals, and foodstuffs. But profits were slow at New Helvetia—until early 1848 when sawmill builder Marshall discovered gold. News of this was communicated to Sutter, who traveled to the site and determined to keep the matter secret. However, when a teamster took a nugget found along the mill trace to the C.C. Smith store and tried to purchase a bottle of brandy with it, the cat was out of the bag. Smith informed Brannan. Quick to seize the opportunity, Brannan and Smith stocked their store with everything necessary for a stay in the mountains. Then on May 12, 1848,

Land speculator, merchant, and newspaper publisher Samuel Brannan played a major role in the city's development.

29

Brannan literally shouted the news of the discovery on the streets of San Francisco. The gold rush was launched and so was Brannan's fortune and the city of Sacramento.

As the news spread, Brannan purchased more goods in order to outfit the steady flow of miners coming up the Sacramento River. The shop at New Helvetia was too small and too removed from the patterns of movement up the river, so Brannan and another associate, P.B. Cornwall, sought to relocate to a more strategic location and appealed to developer Lansford Hastings for free land in Sutterville. In exchange, Brannan held out the tantalizing prospect of future riches for all involved when his warehouse and shop would become the economic hub of the new community. But, because of previous dealings, Hastings was mistrustful of Brannan and refused the offer. Brannan then moved up the Sacramento River to the foot of modern K Street and claimed a small clearing cleaned out by Sutter's men for use as a boat landing, called Sutter's Embarcadero. On this spot, he simply overrode the claims of previous occupant George McDougal, who there ran a ferry service across the Sacramento. Brannan erected a few tents and set up shop alongside the river. By this simple act, Brannan established the location of the present-day city of Sacramento, for around this

Sam Brannan relocated his store to Sacramento's early embarcadero, quickly putting up this frame storehouse at Front and J Streets.

wilderness embarcadero, a new community would arise. The site, however, would have its problems. As historian Mark Eifler noted, Sutterville enjoyed a geographically better position, safely secure from periodic flooding. Nonetheless, Brannan's command of goods and capital exercised a defining role. Despite its being in a flood plain, the strategically located embarcadero trumped any fears generated by Mother Nature; it had a better claim by virtue of what Eifler called the "geography of trade."

Hundreds and then thousands—nearly 6,000 alone in the summer and fall of 1848—came to the embarcadero, tethered their schooners in the still-deep waters of the river, and jumped off to begin the trek into the gold country. With them came more merchants, entertainers, gamblers, and people who, like Brannan, were looking to capitalize on this mighty rush. Brannan made as much as $5,000 a day, almost all of which was sheer profit. In the midst of it all, Sutter, who actually owned the land on the embarcadero, left the burgeoning community just as it was beginning to make money. In fact he was in debt to Brannan (as he was to many people in the valley), who seized a precious opportunity to solidify his claims to this lucrative location. In the fall of 1848, Sutter's long-abandoned son, John Sutter, Jr., arrived at the fort, anxious to meet up with his father. The solemn younger Sutter soon discovered that his father had many debts and little liquid capital. When the elder Sutter delegated to his son the "honor" of straightening out his tangled finances (and promptly left for the Coloma gold site with a gang of Indian peons), Brannan was ready to pounce. With the assistance of another fort merchant, Samuel Hensley, he pressed young Sutter to hire engineers to survey and plat Sutter's holdings and to plan a new city that would begin at the embarcadero. City lots could be sold to retire the debts.

Brannan's suggestions were really the best since the land stretching east from the river was now in high demand. Young Sutter gave his approval and agreed to name the new community "Sacramento City." In late December 1848, Hensley and Sutter Jr. secured the services of Peter H. Burnett, a lawyer who had migrated from Missouri to Oregon and taken an active hand in the formation of territorial government. Burnett had come to California in September 1848 but, like many, found mining distasteful. He arrived at Sutter's Fort just when he was most needed. When they offered the attorney one-fourth of the gross proceeds from the sale of the lots, he snapped at it.

In December 1848, Sutter Jr. commissioned Captain William H. Warner, an army engineer, and his assistants, Lieutenants William Tecumseh Sherman and Edward O.C. Ord, to survey and plat the new city. A traditional American grid pattern was superimposed on the lands from the river east to just beyond Sutter's Fort and south from Sutter's Slough—a finger of the Sacramento River extending inland to Sixth Street between I Street and the American River. East-west streets bore the letters of the alphabet while north-south streets had numbers. The street along the river was Front Street. Young Sutter donated alleys and streets as well as space for ten public parks. The city was now "packaged" for sale, and a land rush began in earnest.

31

CREATING SACRAMENTO CITY

Even before Warner's survey of the city, the embarcadero exploded with life as miners turned it into the starting point for their march to the gold fields. Sacramento's first business establishments were ships tied up along the riverside. These vessels, along with the makeshift tents of Brannan and others, served nascent Sacramento as stores, freight warehouses, jails, and even water purification centers. Samuel Hensley and Pierson B. Reading put up the first frame building on the corner of Front and I Streets. Brannan quickly put up a frame storehouse at Front and J. By early April 1848, 12 simple buildings rose near the busy embarcadero and hundreds of eager immigrants bought their supplies as they moved through. The sale of the lots began in January 1849, just as the pace of gold fever was accelerating.

Optimistic miners and merchants who hoped to "mine the miners" descended on Sacramento from every direction. Overland emigrant groups, weary and weather-beaten, tramped over the Sierras and camped in Sacramento. Ships that had come past Cape Horn disgorged their passengers in San Francisco who then transferred to sloops or schooners that moved up the river to Sacramento. Brannan and his competitors Hensley and Reading purchased sailing vessels to transport goods and people to Sacramento. Steamboats began chugging up the river. By 1850, two sailing ships unloaded their passengers every day. Mules and wagons hauled people and goods to the gold fields. The paths of those early gold rush trails brought miners down a primitive J Street where they turned left on 12th Street and then forded the American River by Lisle's Ferry, later Lisle's Bridge, the site of the present 16th Street Bridge. From there they headed for the American, Bear, Yuba, and Feather Rivers. Other roads led to the mines, including present-day Stockton, Folsom, and Auburn Boulevards and Marysville Road. Before they went, they stopped and shopped at the busy emporia along the river. J and K Streets became an important commercial area. At Sixth and K, a Horse Market also thrived. Brannan and his associates went forward and created the three-story City Hotel out of an old flour mill they had disassembled from an inland Sutter-held site and rebuilt on the riverfront.

Many of the early businesses were housed in large canvas tents, some salvaged from the sails of abandoned vessels. The first church building in the city was the Baltimore Chapel of the Methodist Episcopal Church, made of pre-fabricated materials brought around the Horn. James Lee pitched an early tent structure that provided space for gambling and other entertainment on J Street. The smell of urine and feces from the drinkers and gamblers in the large, damp canvas led to the legendary sobriquet "The Stinking Tent." Gambling halls, bars, restaurants, and houses of prostitution were important pieces of Sacramento's early social life.

Gold rush era Sacramento was a challenging place to live. Forty-niner James Winchester wrote to his relatives in mid-1849:

Sacramento City contains more than ten thousand inhabitants. Most of the stores and houses are without floors, with canvas roofs and walls. No building is enclosed by a fence; but all are, as it were, in one immense open lot, one great cesspool of mud, offal, garbage, dead animals and that worst of nuisances consequent upon the entire absence of outhouses. I can't describe it as it is, but it is desolate beyond description.

Since living conditions could get no worse, things did improve. The number of residences grew steadily, first simple frame structures and later more sturdy brick houses. Society and local culture became increasingly more "respectable" as one of Sacramento's first civic events, a large Fourth of July ball held in 1849, took place in the partially completed city hotel.

Sacramento's emergence on the embarcadero was not assured without some struggle. Stung by Brannan's arrogant disregard of his own prior rights on the riverfront, rival George McDougal attempted to halt the development of the new community. He rousted Sutter from his Coloma hideaway and brought him back to take control of the enterprise. Sutter was powerless to do much except fire Burnett, who in return for his fees demanded and received a large number of city lots. McDougal claimed that he had leasing rights to a large portion of the embarcadero. Hence, efforts to build on this leased land would have to be halted. Sutter Jr., at Brannan's urging, contested this "claim" in court and McDougal's lease was thrown out. McDougal also attempted to shift commercial dominance to Sutterville by offering to sell his supply of goods at cost in order to undercut the embarcadero merchants. Further, he induced Lansford Hastings and Sutter to

Artist J. Cameron created this view of an encampment in early Sacramento (lithographed by G.V. Cooper in 1849).

33

offer 80 free lots to lure merchants to Sutterville. Brannan and his cronies replied with violence, destroying McDougal's goods and then turning to Sutter Jr. to up the ante on free land. With more land to give, Sutter Jr. offered the merchants 500 lots. Sutterville slumped into oblivion, except for a brewery and a brick works.

John Sutter Sr. retired to his property at Hock Farm on the Yuba River. When an arsonist destroyed his property, he spent the remainder of his life alternately reminiscing about early days in Sacramento and petitioning the U.S. government for recompense for his lost lands. He moved east to Lititz, Pennsylvania and, after the failure of his last petition to Congress, died on June 18, 1880.

Sacramento's early economy and its future were fueled by capital investment. People put money in and did what they could to make sure the money earned a profit. Brannan typified this spirit of entrepreneurial self-interest that helped to shape the city. He became the leading merchant, buying land for speculation and erecting buildings for his own use and to lease out to others. Brannan and other capitalists like him invested in the future of Sacramento's embarcadero location and the projection of a commercial district along J and K Streets. These men were the first wave of successful businessmen who made their money by "mining the miners." The firms of Hensley, Reading & Company and Priest, Lee & Company had also begun at Sutter's Fort. For a time both equipped individual miners, but eventually Barton Lee (of Priest, Lee), one of Sacramento's wealthiest men, edged out Hensley by concentrating on the wholesale trade and leaving retailing to smaller operators. Any speculator with capital could inflate land prices. Sutter Jr. insisted on a $250 cap on lot sales, but once the lots were sold at that minimal price, their value increased considerably.

John Sutter Jr. hired engineers to survey and plan a new city that would begin at the embarcadero.

FORGING A GOVERNMENT, SETTLING COMPETING CLAIMS

People with an active stake in Sacramento's economic future also played a key role in devising and planning stable city institutions. Assuring urban order was another way of protecting investments. Although population patterns followed no predictable formula, Sacramento's numbers generally ebbed and flowed with the rhythms of the mining seasons. During the dry months, the city emptied as its inhabitants trudged the mountains looking for gold. In the wet winter months, Sacramento filled with people waiting for the rains to cease and the streams to become workable again. More inhabitants meant more merchants who settled in the city to provide more products and services for the miners. More investment in the city meant more interest in providing a stable government and assuring order in the sometimes disorderly community.

Inherent class tensions increased among early Sacramentans as patterns of land ownership emerged. Most immigrants arrived with hope but little cash. With the great demand for land, real estate prices began to command higher prices. Lots that had initially sold for $250 were now marketed for $8,000. Consequently, those who owned more land soon rose to the top of an economic aristocracy. One group of men, defined by historian Mark Eifler as the "great speculators," acquired the resources to hold substantial real estate. According to his research, about one-fourth of the residents of the city held property, but the bulk of those holdings consisted of only one lot. Most Sacramentans were renters or transients who owned nothing. Of the others, 100 owned at least two lots, 42 owned at least $20,000 in property, and 21 held more than $50,000. This loose coalition of merchants, traders, and speculators were the movers and shakers and the most insistent about creating government entities to protect their rights.

The origins of Sacramento's first city government are not altogether clear. Under Mexican law, Sutter had held the position of *alcalde* (a term with no precise English equivalent to describe its duties but it combined executive, legislative, and judicial functions in one person). In September 1846, John Sinclair was elected magistrate of the Sacramento District. The situation grew muddled after Mexican law and military rule formally ended in May 1848 when Congress approved the Treaty of Guadalupe Hidalgo. The U.S. Congress had anticipated organizing a California territory shortly after the Mexican War, but the issue of California's admission to the Union got snared in the escalating debate over the extension of slavery. The matter would not be resolved until late summer of 1850 when the last of the sectional compromises that kept the Union together would be forged in Congress, and California was admitted as a free state. But between the start of the gold rush and California's admission to the Union in September 1850, the pressing needs for social order and stability grew more intense as the gold rush telescoped the "normal" time line of growth and social development into a relatively short space. Sacramento needed a stable government but lurched toward it with uncertainty and some conflict.

In early 1849, a group of merchants laid out a simple government structure for Sacramento County consisting of a sheriff and an alcalde. John Frederick Morse, a physician who wrote one of the first histories of the city, noted that elections had already taken place in late 1848 for two alcaldes. In a more romantic version, Morse describes the first laws of Sacramento being crafted at a meeting under a spreading oak tree at the foot of I Street in the spring of 1849. A territory-wide election in August 1849 to select delegates to a state constitutional convention was called, which gave the umbrella for the election of Sacramento's first city council. William Stout became the first mayor and when Stout left town, General A.M. Winn, a land agent, replaced him. The council consisted largely of the wealthiest men in the city, including Sam Brannan, Barton Lee, John McDougal, and Samuel Hensley.

These councilmen set up a series of committees to deal with specific areas of urban need: finances, the waterfront, roads, and a city center. They also set to drafting a charter, which initially voters rejected, in part because of proposed prohibitions against gambling. In October, a second charter election was held, and this time the document succeeded. The newly formed California Legislature accepted the charter in February 1850, the first in California, and the city officially commenced on March 18, 1850. A new city council was elected on April 1 and Hardin Bigelow, a local businessman, became the first mayor under this new charter.

THE PERILOUS YEAR: 1850

Sacramento's first official year of existence was its most perilous. On the front burner was the growing dispute over property rights. The clash between land developers—who had indeed played an important role in creating the new city despite natural disasters—and the landless (and those who held little land) may not have been inevitable, but it did come. The city's real estate was falling under the control of a core of well-endowed capitalists with the funds to purchase large numbers of lots, parcels that were often subdivided and sold at higher prices or used as collateral to purchase needed inventory for shops and stores. However, questions surfaced about the legality of Sutter's land grant. The federal government empowered a land commission to begin the arduous process of evaluating the validity of all the Mexican grants, so Sutter's New Helvetia grant, plagued by the imperfect lines drawn by Vioget, was one of the first to come under scrutiny.

As the city flooded with miners, especially overland immigrants who needed a place to stay, extensive landowners began charging the weary newcomers nightly fees to camp on their lands. Some of these came with sharply etched ideas about their rights under government pre-emption policies and began to deeply resent the monopolization of land in and around Sacramento. In the middle of October 1850, one Z.M. Chapman built a log dwelling on a vacant lot outside the city limits near Sutter's Fort. Representatives of Priest, Lee & Company visited the enterprising Chapman and informed him that he had to stop building since their company owned the property. When Chapman refused, a court case was launched and the doughty woodsman insisted that the company show evidence of ownership. When they were unable to do so to his satisfaction, Chapman challenged the Sutter claim on which the company based its ownership and then called into question all city land titles. Emboldened by this, a wave of squatters began to sink roots on city lands. The squatters themselves formed an organization called the Sacramento City Settlers Association. A Massachusetts physician, Dr. Charles Robinson, became its president and the intellectual wellspring of the movement. Robinson not only vigorously endorsed Chapman's claim, but he also built his own squatter's cabin near the levee.

Naturally, landowners, led by Brannan, upheld the legality of Sutter's claim and mobilized against the squatters. Strongly represented on the city council, the landowners decried Robinson's provocative action and had the shanty torn down. The destruction of the Robinson structure might have set off tensions right away, but floods drove the transients out of Sacramento in the winter of 1849–1850 and this brought a temporary end to the problems. Moreover, the opening of the placer mines in the spring further emptied the city. However, slowly but surely the transients made their way back—many of them weary of the slim pickings in the gold fields and others looking for a place to settle, dry out, and relax. The settlers' organization did its best to keep alive the question of the validity of Sutter's grant. A controversial and widely disseminated pamphlet by John Plumbe argued vigorously that Sutter's claim, which now encompassed the city limits, was questionable. Sutter was himself, in the logic of the pamphlet, a squatter. With renewed vigor, squatters again began to settle on undeveloped Sacramento land, and the landowners hit back. Aided by an April 1850 law passed by the transitional state legislature, "An Act concerning forcible entry and Unlawful Detainer," they

Land agent and brigadier general, A.M. Winn was one of Sacramento's early mayors.

now had the legal authority to eject squatters. Their next move was to have a city ordinance passed forbidding the building of tents, shanties, or houses on any vacant lot belonging to a private person. The landowners also formed a Law and Order Association.

Anxious to test the new laws, city council member John P. Rogers brought suit against squatter John T. Madden, who had settled on a vacant lot on the corner of Second and N Streets. Madden found himself hauled before the newly organized recorder's court, which had jurisdiction over city ordinances. Judge B.F. Washington ruled against Madden, who promptly appealed the decision to a county court. Squatters and landowners then squared off in their respective organizations. One of the loudest voices in defense of the squatters was a young Irish immigrant, James McClatchy, whose militant rhetoric urged squatters to active resistance. When County Judge E.J. Willis ruled against Madden's appeal on August 10, 1850, the stage was set for violence. McClatchy and fellow squatter supporter Michael Moran were arrested by city authorities and charged with resisting or attempting to resist the sheriff who was trying to get Madden off the contested lot. Arrest warrants for other squatter sympathizers, including the militant Robinson, also went forth.

Four days later, fighting erupted when a band of settlers (perhaps 40 or 50) led by Robinson and James Maloney attempted to re-take Madden's claim. As their rag-tag band marched through the heart of the city, local officials thought the group intended to spring McClatchy and Moran. When this did not happen, Mayor Hardin Bigelow and Sheriff Joseph McKinney ordered them to disperse. At the corner of Fourth and J, the long simmering hostility exploded as shots were fired. Bigelow was wounded four times and city assessor J.W. Woodland, standing near Bigelow, was killed. Other casualties included one of the settlers, a small boy standing nearby, and one of the citizens. Maloney's horse was shot out from under him, and he was pursued and shot to death in an alley. Robinson, wounded in the leg, was arrested. General A.M. Winn, head of the city council, invoked martial law and recruited 500 volunteers to keep order. The following day, Sheriff McKinney and a posse tracked down a dozen settlers at the Five Mile House in Brighton. In another gunfight, McKinney and three settlers were killed.

The episode, so traumatic and dramatic, has often been told as a tale of good versus evil—land speculators versus the democratic land equalizers. In part this is true, but in reality the issues are far more complex and reveal important class tensions that marked the city during its formative era. In the end, the bitter standoff redoubled the efforts of civic leaders to create more stability. Eventually the federal government upheld the Sutter grant and the speculators won. In some respects, the victory of the landholders was temporary. Their efforts to use Sacramento as a speculative enterprise eventually gave way to a more welcoming attitude toward newcomers. Land and settlement in Sacramento needed to be opened up, not restricted to the profiteering motives of a relative few. The bitter experiences with land monopoly in Sacramento framed the life and career of James McClatchy, destined to be a major force in city journalism.

Squatters riot in Sacramento City.

FLOODS, FIRES, AND EPIDEMICS

The decision to locate Sacramento on the embarcadero may have been an economically sound one, but the location had some serious problems. Anxious to secure their economic foothold, Brannan and others did not give much attention to the fact that the land was very low. They may even have ignored the bits and pieces of driftwood around the site and even in the trees—signs that the area was sometimes under water. Indeed, Sacramento was prone to flooding, and a primitive levee hastily erected along the embarcadero was inadequate. Heavy rains in late 1849 extended into January 1850. On January 8, the American River burst into the city, sweeping away virtually everything in its path. Future mayor Hardin Bigelow urged the building of higher levees, advice that was only heeded in the spring when the Sierra snowpack melted and the rivers rose again. Bigelow's makeshift levee held back the next torrent. On April 29, Sacramentans voted to tax themselves $250,000 to build a levee to encircle the city. Only 3 feet high, 6 feet wide at the top, and 12 feet wide at the base, the earthwork was a first effort to alter the liabilities entailed in Sacramento's location. But in 1852, these modest levees failed, and floods again inundated the city. In response, local landowner Samuel Norris laid out a nice, neat little town called Hoboken (near what is today the J Street entrance to California State University), and for six weeks about 1,000 people found refuge there. Prospects looked bright for Norris's town and steamers plied their way to the new site with supplies. However, once the waters receded, Hoboken slipped into oblivion. Sacramentans gave no thought to moving the city to higher ground but set to

Early Sacramento City was prone to flooding.

work building higher levees. Before it was over, Sacramentans spent nearly $600,000 protecting their city from floods.

Water would be an enemy in other ways as well. On October 18, 1850, a steamship bringing news of California statehood to Sacramento also carried passengers with the dreaded cholera. Before the epidemic ran its course, nearly 600 died and many more fled. Dr. John Frederick Morse, one of the city's first physicians and chroniclers, referred to Sacramento during those months as "a veritable lazar house." Hundreds died and were buried in the city cemetery, donated by John Sutter on the southern fringe of the city, now Tenth and Broadway.

Although floods and disease were serious threats to Sacramento's well-being, its counterpart, fire, did just as much damage until it too was controlled. Early Sacramento was a tinder box, with many of its structures made of canvas tent material or framed with dried-out pine lumber. Long dry summers raised the potential for fire, and in September 1849 the city was wiped out by a blaze—a harbinger of future conflagrations. In mid-1850, the *annus horribilis* of Sacramento's existence, another roaring blaze destroyed again the canvas and flimsy wooden structures. On November 4, 1852, by the time Sacramento had begun to develop a more settled "urban look" with large buildings, streets, and a distinct commercial district, fire broke out in Madame Lanos's millinery shop near Fourth and J Streets. Fanned by a strong north wind, the blaze destroyed 55 blocks. Two years later, another destructive fire hit in the scalding month of July. Between 1855 and 1870, fire ravaged the city periodically. This impelled a steady improvement in the quality of its fire services, creating two new volunteer companies, but the city did not have a full-time, paid fire department until 1872.

As with the water crisis, the collective forces of urban regeneration invoked the spirit if not the letter of *Urbs Indomita* and rebuilt the city soon after the ashes cooled. Brick structures soon began to dot the streets (in 1855, the city passed an ordinance mandating them in the business district). Indeed, by 1856, Sacramento had 500 brick (built with materials manufactured in one of the 30 brick yards around the city) and 2,000 frame buildings. Major hotels and gathering places included the Golden Eagle at Seventh and K, the Clarendon on Second, the Dawson House, later known as the St. George, at Fourth and J, and the What Cheer House at Front and K Streets. Other industries included breweries, soda water manufacturers, and two iron and brass foundries.

BUILDING A STATE CAPITOL

The early process of city building reached a pivotal moment when the state government decided to locate California's wandering state capital in Sacramento in 1854. California's constitutional convention met at Colton Hall in the old Mexican capital of Monterey. The subject of the permanent seat of California's capital had been taken up and for a time it was decided to locate it in San Jose. However, when San Jose proved unready for the new government, a bidding war was set off among a number of California cities—including San Luis Obispo and Santa Barbara in the south and Benicia, Stockton, San Francisco, and Vallejo in the northern part of the state. Sacramento had also placed a bid and, in fact, had served as temporary quarters in 1852 while Vallejo, the choice for a time, readied itself. The first Sacramento courthouse hosted the legislature in January 1852, but the city's chances to hold the temporary capital evaporated when flooding hit, and the legislators migrated to Benicia. Although the legislature had capacious quarters there, the town proved too small for state government. Sacramento then made another bid. In January 1854, the mayor and common council offered the legislature and state officers free use of their handsome new courthouse, fireproof vaults for public money and records, and removal from Benicia to Sacramento without charge. The city further sweetened the pot by granting the state a public square between I and J and Ninth and Tenth Streets for a permanent capitol.

Legislators may have worried about Sacramento's climate and propensity to be wiped off the map, but they also admired the city's willingness to rebuild. They were also probably attracted by the city's various entertainments and abundant hotels. Sacramento boasted 55 hotels, planked streets, 14 stages, and 28 river steamers. In February 1854, Senator Amos Parnall Catlin, a longtime advocate of Sacramento, introduced a bill to fix the permanent location of the government in Sacramento. The bill passed both houses, and on February 25, Governor John Bigler signed it into law. When the courthouse was destroyed in the fire of 1854, a newer and even more capacious building was erected in anticipation of the legislature's relocation in January 1855. The state paid

$12,000 a year for the Sacramento courthouse, and it served as the hub of California government until 1869.

On March 15, 1856, Senator William J. Ferguson introduced a bill to issue bonds to construct a new state capitol. Work actually began on a Greek-style building, but stopped after two weeks when state officers decided the bond issue violated the state constitution. The project sat for a while, and San Francisco, Oakland, and San Jose pitched hard to secure the capital for their cities. Nonetheless, in 1860, Sacramento trumped its rivals by offering the state new land between L and N, Tenth and Twelfth Streets. Governor John Downey signed a bill appropriating $500,000 for a capitol building project, and the design submitted by Miner Frederick Butler was accepted. However, before it could get underway, Sacramento was hit by serious flooding in 1861–1862, raising again the prospect of capital removal. The legislature adjourned temporarily to San Francisco but was back in January 1863. The construction of the capitol resumed in June, and although it would not be entirely completed until 1874, it was ready for occupancy in November 1869.

Constructed of brick with facades, outer steps, and columns, of granite from California quarries, the capitol covered an area of 52,480 square feet, cost nearly $2.6 million, and resembled the U.S. capitol. The structure was shaped like an "E" with the arms facing east and was capped by a 125-foot dome, the most important feature of Sacramento's skyline for many years. All the offices of state government and the legislature were contained within the new building. The legislature formally took possession of its respective chambers on December 6, 1869. It is still the most elegant building in the city and a natural benchmark for urban excellence. In 1866, a writer for the *Evening Bee* expressed in poetic fashion the hope that the new building would bring a defining presence to Sacramento: "It is a masterful piece of architecture. . . . The effect it will have on the taste and

A new county court house served as the state capitol from 1855 to 1869.

Construction of the California state capitol building was interrupted by serious flooding in 1861–1862.

manners and morality of our city will be almost incredible. No man will be able to look upon it and not feel its refining impulses."

Around the grounds of the capitol, a beautiful public park was laid out with handsome granite pillars marking the access paths to the statehouse. The business of state government was initially slow, with the legislature meeting biennially and for only short periods. Some state offices, like the Supreme Court, eventually moved to San Francisco, but the capital remained firmly ensconced in Sacramento. For Sacramento, the state proved to be an extremely stable employer. The number of jobs has grown steadily and has only slightly been offset by boom and bust cycles. The presence of government employees in Sacramento has historically provided it with a cadre of well-educated and cultured men and women who have supported good education and cultural development.

By constitutional amendment in 1861, Sacramento became the permanent home of the annual state fair. Housed for many years in the State Agricultural Pavilion on Sixth and M Streets and on 43 acres of prime city property called Union Park (today the Boulevard Park neighborhood), it also included a popular race track. The state fair brought an annual stream of visitors to the state capital and provided a substantial boost to the local economy. In 1906, it was moved to an 80-acre site on Stockton Boulevard.

THE CREATION OF URBAN COMMUNITY

Sacramento continued the process of community building throughout the 1850s. As the highly-individualistic "easy pickings" of the placer fields gave way to the more labor intensive and expensive hard rock and hydraulic mining, more people moved to Sacramento and devoted themselves to urban life.

Demographically, Sacramento had always been a diverse place. Most gold rush denizens hailed from eastern states and often gathered together in state groupings to maintain contact with one another. Irish settlers were quite prominent in early Sacramento, many of them emigrating from Irish enclaves in the eastern states. Irish denizens brought with them a love for the old land and a hearty Irish patriotism, as well as an attachment to the Catholic Church. The Irish in Sacramento found their natural home in St. Rose of Lima Church at Seventh and K Streets, which they dominated for many years. Irish priests and nuns provided an important core of literate and competent leaders. Irish culture was perpetuated in Sacramento through public celebration, especially of Ireland's patron St. Patrick, and fund-raising and agitation for Irish nationalism were continuous. A number of leading Irish nationalists of the nineteenth century visited Sacramento enroute to San Francisco. The two Catholic schools conducted by Irish nuns and Christian Brothers were bastions of Irish nationalism as students learned Irish history, recited Irish poetry in closing exercises, and celebrated Irish holidays.

Other ethnic groups included German-speaking Swiss, like Sutter, and Germans. Small numbers of Hispanic Californians were also present in early Sacramento. Likewise, a contingent of Native Americans lived in the city. African Americans made their presence felt in the burgeoning city as well. Some made for

St. Rose of Lima Church, shown here c. 1868, provided a natural home for Sacramento's Irish immigrants.

the gold fields, but like others many remained in Sacramento and offered services to transient miners. Sacramento's African-American population, like the Irish, tended to coalesce around its church, the African Methodist Episcopal (AME) Church, the oldest independent African-American denomination. In 1850, St. Andrew's African Methodist Episcopal Church was organized after an earlier attempt had failed. Services were held in the home of Daniel Blue under the leadership of Barney and Daniel Fletcher. Shortly after, a Baptist church, Siloam (later Shiloh), began under the direction of Charles Satchell, holding services in a Chinese Baptist Church on Sixth and H Streets. In May 1854, Elizabeth Thorne Scott opened her home as a school to 14 African-American children. The next year, Reverend Jeremiah Sanderson, a black educator and abolitionist, came from San Francisco and moved the school to facilities offered by the AME Church.

Chinese residents also came in quest of gold. Targeted for discrimination from the first, Chinese miners lost a share of their hard-earned diggings to a noxious foreign miners tax that was passed to dissuade the Chinese from competing with American-born miners. As a result, the Chinese immigrants learned to provide services to urban Sacramento and were ghettoized. Chinese Sacramentans settled along I Street, near "China Slough" (also known as Sutter Slough), forming one of the first distinct ethnic enclaves in the city. Chinese restaurants, gambling establishments, and businesses (especially laundries) popped up in this section of town. Almost exclusively male, Chinese residents slowly welcomed a growing female population. The number of Chinese steadily grew in the city, numbering nearly 1,200 by 1860.

Although issues of class and economic difference continued to surface throughout the city's history, the so-called "civic middlemen" described by historian Mark Eifler stepped forward to even out sharp class differences and provide a solid middle class. These merchants included those who made a living carting goods—teamsters and river line operators. Likewise, physicians were part of this guild of solid citizens, having burnished their credentials in the disastrous cholera epidemic of 1850 and occupying important roles in the city's growing concern for public health. The city's religious leaders, members of the press, and teachers were vital parts of that "civic middle" in that they had significant influence on public opinion. Invested in the city and anxious to provide for its greater advancement and development, these middlemen bridged the gap between the urban working class and the great speculators, providing a solid community with leadership in civic office and social affairs and also making accessible the resources of the city to those who aspired to their status. These groups centered their activities symbolically in the bustling trade along the embarcadero and also near the Horse Market.

WOMEN'S ROLES

The forging of deeper community ties was also facilitated by the increasing presence of women. With its raucous gaming tables and hoop-ti-do gold rush ribaldry, Sacramento seemed an uncongenial place for many nineteenth-century

Chinese Sacramentans settled along I Street, forming one of the first distinct ethnic enclaves in the city.

women whose social training excluded such "unrespectable" entertainment. The 1850 census noted that only 6.96 percent of the 6,820 inhabitants of Sacramento were women (475 women to 6,345 men). The gendered world of Sacramento grew steadily, bringing with it a stability that moved the city beyond its hurly-burly origins. Women in early Sacramento did indeed speak of their efforts to tame the wild miners, but they also set themselves to earn a living. Women ran hotels and restaurants, but according to historians Dian Self and Elaine Connolly, the majority of women employed outside the home earned their livelihood in the clothing trade. Other jobs like housekeeping, millinery, and midwifery were also available to Sacramento women. One brave woman, Mrs. John Zwicker, operated a saloon and shooting gallery at Third and J.

Two important aspects of women's life represented opposite ends of the moral spectrum: prostitution and the convent. Although viewed as a moral vice (and one that city leaders periodically railed against but never seriously tried to eliminate), prostitution provided another source of income for enterprising women. The "world's oldest profession" apparently enjoyed an open field for many years, and ladies of the night were seldom arrested. One prominent madam, Johanna Hiegel, ran a cigar business and a house of prostitution on Second between I and J for nearly 30 years beginning in 1854.

Another breed of dedicated and enterprising women, the Roman Catholic Sisters of Mercy, appeared in Sacramento in October 1857 and set to work educating the young and caring for the homebound. Later, they would become prominent providers of health care. This community exercised their religious life in a distinctive way—wearing special garb, living celibate lives in community, and having enormous influence in business and educational affairs, perhaps more than any other group of Sacramento women. In 1860, they opened St. Joseph's Academy for girls, a school that took in grade school to young adult women of all religious denominations and trained them in classical subjects as well as in more practical domestic duties. Their first convent was planned for the same site that was later claimed by the state capitol. Forced to move when the city gave the land to the state, the sisters opened their large convent at Eighth and G Streets and remained there with their school until the late 1960s. The sisters exercised an important role in the distribution of charity. Visiting the homes of the poor and destitute, educating the young, and providing relief in disasters were just a few of the ways in which the Sisters of Mercy endeared themselves to the wider population of Sacramento.

RELIGIOUS INSTITUTIONS

The presence of the Sisters of Mercy highlights the role of religion in shaping Sacramento's early culture. As in many areas overwhelmed by a flood of foot-loose young men in search of gold, organized religion of any sort had a hard time gaining traction in Sacramento. Optimism did burn bright, however. Since the area around Sacramento had not been missionized by Roman Catholics, Protestant evangelicals anxious to win "God's gold" moved quickly to claim the area. Reverend Sylvester Woolbridge, a representative of the old school Presbyterians, preached the first "sermon" on the Sacramento riverbank in the spring of 1848. Other ministers began in temporary quarters and some took to preaching on the levee. Methodist-Episcopalian pastor W. Grove Deal began the first regular religious services in May 1849. Sacramento's most famous minister was Joseph Augustine Benton, a Congregational minister who did not come originally to preach the gospel but to mine gold. When this failed in early 1849, he took up residence in Sacramento, founding the First Church of Christ in September 1849 and remained for nearly ten years, longer than any other minister in the city during the gold rush era. Notably eloquent, Benton played an important role as a religious leader and a public citizen. Benton's castle-like church, first erected on Sixth Street, was designed by local architect Albion Sweetser and became a popular lecture and music hall for Sacramento. Sacramento's Republican Party held its first convention in the church.

However, despite their best efforts, the promotion of Sabbath observance in early Sacramento was frustrating. John Morse's history notes, "Sunday was almost a forgotten day. . . ." But gradually more ministers came and with them more stable congregations. Methodists had established themselves early on in Sacramento. Indeed, Sacramento's first church building was put up in 1849 by Methodist preacher Isaac Owens, the Baltimore Chapel located at Seventh and L Streets. Methodists later put up the city's first brick church on Seventh Street. Baptist and Episcopal churches followed. In August 1850, Dominican Father Peter Anderson founded St. Rose of Lima Church on lots donated by Catholic convert and first governor Peter Burnett. Chinese inhabitants worshiped at the Chinese Baptist Church on Sixth and H, but most retained their own Buddhist rituals. Sacramento had its own Joss House in the Chinese district. Religion, it was felt, tended to tame "a most vitiated and chaotic community." The common struggles of religious leaders in early Sacramento produced a kind of practical ecumenism. Church members of various denominations contributed to the building funds of others. Non-Catholics sent their sons and daughters to Catholic schools. Sometimes inter-denominational kindness had a hook. For example, the Baltimore Chapel was loaned to Sacramento's fledgling Jewish community for its High Holy days "so that the spirit of the building would bring them back to the true religion." Jewish Sacramentans did not become Christians, but they did purchase the chapel to house Congregation B'Nai Israel in June 1852.

THE PRESS

As religious institutions helped create a more stable community, so also did the rise of a popular press. Samuel Brannan backed editor Edward C. Kemble in issuing the city's first paper, *Placer Times*, on April 28, 1849. Located at the fort, it moved to the Front Street location on July 9, 1849 and covered some of the first events of city life. In April 1850, a second newspaper, the *Sacramento Transcript* commenced. In all, 44 newspapers came and went between 1849 and 1858, but only two remained: the *Sacramento Union* and the *Sacramento Daily Bee*. The *Union*, the eldest of the two papers, had begun in 1851 when a rate war between the *Placer Times* and the *Transcript* resulted in a pay cut for the printers. The *Union* continued until January 1994. It would change ownership and editorial direction many times.

The evening *Sacramento Daily Bee* began when the *California American* went out of existence. Owned by a consortium of businessmen, Levi C. Chandler, William H. Tobey, John Church, and Lyman P. Davis, the *Bee's* first editor was Cherokee poet John Rollin Ridge. Ridge lasted only a few months and was replaced by another prominent local journalist, James McClatchy. A native of Ireland's County Antrim, McClatchy had come to the United States in 1840, settling first in New York, where he became associated with Horace Greeley's *New York Tribune*. Perhaps hearkening to Greeley's famed injunction to "Go west young man and grow up with the country," McClatchy migrated to California via a harrowing trip through Mexico and up the California coast. After a brief stint in the mining fields, he settled in Sacramento in the late summer of 1849. From the beginning, McClatchy interested himself in the welfare and future of Sacramento and became deeply involved in virtually every aspect of its development. He joined in a number of journalistic endeavors and also in local politics, writing for the *Placer Times, Democratic State Journal,* and the *Californian.* Once he replaced Ridge, McClatchy remained linked with the *Bee*, only taking off time to become Sacramento sheriff between 1864 and 1866 and for a brief stint working at a San Francisco paper. His interest in the *Bee* gradually evolved into a partnership with others and eventually, sole ownership of the paper. By the time of his death in 1883, he was able to turn the paper over to his two sons, Charles Kenny and Valentine, who secured family dominance over Sacramento journalism down to the present.

The Sacramento Bee *was located on Third between J and K Streets.*

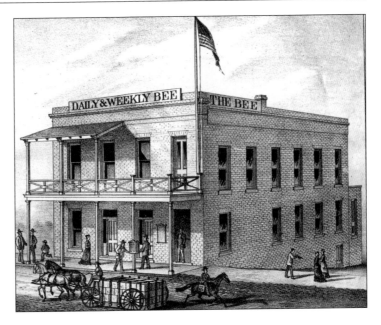

SCHOOLS AND OTHER ELEMENTS OF COMMUNITY

Schools also contributed to the development of community. It took time for public schools to emerge since private institutions moved first to meet the growing demands for education. Already in 1849, Congregationalist minister Joseph Augustine Benton had begun a school under the auspices of his church. Sacramento Methodists formed a successful school as well. By 1852, there were nine private schools. The Sacramento Academy and the Young Ladies Seminary were two of the best known. A Roman Catholic school later associated with the Sisters of Mercy was formed at St. Rose of Lima Church.

On April 26, 1853, the state legislature authorized the Sacramento City Council to establish free common schools, and on February 20, 1854, the first public school (Franklin School) opened at Fifth and K. By July nearly 500 children were attending public and private schools in the Sacramento area. Between 1854 and 1893, the city built and maintained 13 schools. In 1856, Sacramento opened the second high school in California. Sacramento schools were segregated until 1885. In May 1856, a small public school for African-American children was built on Fifth and O Streets.

To accentuate the growing civilization of the city, a public library opened in November 1857, with 800 volumes secured from gifts and an energetic subscription campaign. Likewise, theater was present from the beginning, aligned perhaps to the somewhat bawdy acts in the gambling tents. Sacramento's first theater was a frame and canvas structure crowned by a tin roof called the Eagle Theater. Rowdy miners sat on benches facing the stage, while a modest balcony accessed by ladder was arranged for the ladies. Wiped out in the floods of 1850, the site was sold to new owners, who moved to Second Street and renamed it the Tehama. By the time the Tehama succumbed to the 1851 fire, small theaters and entertainment halls proliferated to meet the needs of lonely and bored transients. One of Sacramento's grandest theaters, the Clunie, built by future Congressman Thomas Jefferson Clunie in 1870 as a hotel, was later enlarged with part of it being converted into a playhouse.

For the hundreds of transients whose life ended here, Sacramento prepared "hallowed ground." The earliest cemetery was started by Sutter near his fort. The land was eventually sold to private developers and is today the site of the Sutter Middle School. The public City Cemetery at Y (Broadway) and Tenth was given to the city by Sutter in 1850 and became Sacramento's prime burial ground. Roman Catholics opened their cemetery south of Y Street in 1860 and Jewish Sacramentans buried their dead at the New Helvetia cemetery at Alhambra and J. Later burial grounds were secured on Stockton Boulevard.

Sacramento had experienced its first tumultuous generation and survived its tenuous location through the sheer determination and strength of its settlers. As a new era dawned Sacramento left behind the early problems of civic disorder, fire and flood, and epidemics.

The first Sacramento High School was located at Ninth and M Streets.

3. A Maturing City

The decade of the 1860s that found most of America caught up in the Civil War presented Sacramento with a reprise of the vulnerabilities inherent in its location. Already in 1853, city leaders had raised the level of I, J, and K Streets, lifting them to the level of the city plaza. They erected new sidewalks and buildings to render them less prone to flooding. However, tremendous flooding in the winter of 1861–1862 created havoc and spurred even greater efforts to protect the city. In 1862, determined city leaders redirected the American River, removing a troublesome curve. They also relieved pressure on the mouth of the American River, bringing it into the Sacramento River at a point about one-fourth of a mile north of the original confluence. Using wheelbarrows and shovels, Sacramentans hauled in dirt from the new channel of the American River to fill in 10-foot high bulkheads along the streets. New wooden sidewalks crowned the streets. Buildings were lifted up by jackscrews and given new foundations. Sometimes first floors of buildings were simply abandoned and second stories became the new entrance. Not all parts of the city had to be raised to the same heights, but by 1873, 12 blocks of I, J, and K Streets were raised as much as 15 feet. In 1877, the first cement sidewalks in Sacramento were laid in Capitol Park under the direction of Adolph Teichert.

Connecting Sacramento to the outside world constituted one of its first important industries. Steamboats coming up from San Francisco plied the waters of the Sacramento. At first a myriad of independent contractors handled this burgeoning business, but eventually the California Steam Navigation Company came to monopolize 75 percent of the river traffic. Ultimately, however, the use of the Sacramento River as an artery of trade and commerce began to falter. Riverboats and other vessels found it difficult to move up the channel due to the large amount of silt and "slickens" that were washed from the mountains into the river by hydraulic miners. Sacramento denizens, led by James McClatchy of the *Bee,* waged a relentless war against the environmental damage done by the "hydraulickers." Legal action came to a head in 1884 when a ruling of the California Supreme Court, the Sawyer Decision, ended the practice.

Teamster companies hauled supplies and mining equipment over the mountains to miners. The Horse Market provided individual riders with animals,

Riverboats plied the waters of the Sacramento River, docking at Sacramento's riverfront, shown here in 1910.

saddles, and harnesses, as well as carriages. Stagecoach travel began in 1849. New Englander James Birch and a partner initiated stage service between Sacramento and Mormon Island. Birch's success opened the field for others. In 1854, Birch and a friend, Frank Stevens, consolidated smaller stage lines into the California Stage Company. At its peak, this firm generated huge profits as it commanded nearly 80 percent of the stage traffic over 3,000 miles of routes connecting major parts of the American West. In 1856, Birch and others pressed Congress to create three wagon roads to the Pacific Coast and approve overland mail from St. Louis to San Francisco. Likewise, the state legislature appropriated funds for the expansion of roads from Sacramento to the state line via Placerville. With roads came telegraph lines that connected Sacramento with Marysville and San Francisco. In 1861, these lines went all the way to Salt Lake City and eventually to the East Coast. Carrying mail via the fabled Pony Express also had a Sacramento connection. The dispatch of these swift couriers lasted only 18 months from 1860 to early 1861, but their romantic appeal of relaying mail across the country from St. Joseph, Missouri to the B.F. Hastings building in Sacramento left a tale repeated from generation to generation and memorialized by a statue in the state historic park in Old Sacramento. However, the Pony Express was quickly replaced by the telegraph.

A DEFINITIVE IMPACT: THE RAILROAD

Sacramento was born just when the railroad was beginning to crisscross America and Congress was debating routes for a major transcontinental system intended to tie the East to the West Coast. The first plans for a railroad in Sacramento date to 1852 when Peter Burnett and others plotted a line that skirted the Sierra foothills to Marysville. Like many infrastructure projects of this magnitude, the project fell apart due to lack of funding. In 1854, another group of entrepreneurs organized the Sacramento Valley Railroad Company (SVRR). While searching for funding sources in the east, the company managed to interest a young engineer, Theodore Judah, who had only recently built a railroad over the Niagara Gorge in New York. From a perch at 31st and M Streets (today Folsom and Alhambra Boulevards), Judah took careful note of the number of mule-driven teams passing from Sacramento into the mountains and realized that a railroad could make a good profit.

Judah plotted a path for a railroad that would plunge into the Sierra Nevada foothills and branch north and south along the base of the mountains. The SVRR track-laying commenced on August 9, 1855, and seven months later, in February 1856, the SVRR officially opened. The rail line began at Third and R and turned east at the R Street levee moving toward Folsom. The 22 miles of tracks cost over $1.3 million but proved their worth by transporting tons of cobblestone and granite for buildings and streets in Sacramento and San Francisco. The discovery of the Comstock Lode in Nevada in 1859 assured the railroad's profitability. Soon a tandem arrangement with the river lines allowed river steamers to haul goods from San Francisco, load them on rail cars, and transfer them to Folsom for distribution to points east in the Sierra Nevada. Reverse shipments brought Comstock silver to Folsom, which was then unloaded in Sacramento and San

Engineer Theodore Judah lobbied for support of a railroad through the towering peaks of the Sierra Nevada.

The first locomotive to operate in California was brought around Cape Horn and put into use by the Sacramento Valley Railroad (photo taken in 1855).

Francisco. According to historian Walter Gray, the chief significance of the SVRR was to demonstrate to Californians the profitability and efficiency of rail travel.

The problem was the Sierra Nevada, which loomed nearly 7,000 feet high at its crest. Judah was fascinated by the challenge of the towering peaks and explored potential routes through them. He even wrote a pamphlet, *A Practical Plan for Building the Pacific Railroad*, and lobbied far and wide for support. Seeking financing, he was dismissed by San Francisco capitalists and others as "Crazy Judah," but their snickering did not deter the young engineer. Turning to Sacramento's increasingly wealthy merchants, he approached four entrepreneurs who had made their livelihood in the state capital—wholesale grocer Leland Stanford (destined to become governor of the state in 1862); his friend, dry goods merchant Charles Crocker; and two hardware retailers, Collis P. Huntington and Mark Hopkins. These four, later known as the "Big Four," met in the upper room of the Stanford Brothers Store, heard Judah, and agreed to underwrite him. Thus, the Central Pacific Railroad was incorporated on June 28, 1861.

Throughout the tumultuous 1850s, Congress had debated the route of a future Pacific railroad and actually pondered several routes across the vast "American Desert." However, the final decision was held hostage to the sectional politics of the 1850s. Once the South withdrew from the Union during the Civil War, Congress approved and President Lincoln signed a bill sanctioning the route cutting through the heart of the country with two railroad companies building from opposite ends. In July 1862, Congress granted the franchise for building the western end to the Central Pacific. Leland Stanford, railroad owner and by then governor of California, provided additional support with state subsidies. (Conflict of interest was not then the issue that it is today.)

Groundbreaking ceremonies for the Central Pacific took place at Front and K Streets on January 8, 1863. With a prayer by Reverend Joseph Augustine Benton and predictions of future prosperity from Governor Stanford and others, the tracks laid in Sacramento moved steadily eastward over the Sierras. Judah never saw the completion of what his imagination helped create. He had broken with the Big Four and died in New England in October 1863.

THE RAILROAD AND SACRAMENTO

It is nearly impossible to exaggerate the importance of the railroad to Sacramento. Railroad building invigorated the economy and increased demand for unskilled labor. Initially, a considerable amount of labor was needed for construction. The rail yards required men and shop workers for their various operations, bringing a host of newcomers to Sacramento. Later, the railroad recruited large gangs of maintenance workers who were needed to keep rail lines open.

Urban demography started to change. Into the older parts of the city came a flood of new residents, mostly immigrants, who worked in the rail yards, in rail-connected industries, and provided services for the growing city: barbers, painters, restaurateurs, and retailers of various sorts. Ethnic groups began to come and arrange themselves mostly in the close-knit neighborhoods on the West End of the city. Although the comparative spatial smallness of Sacramento precluded the development of sharply etched ethnic enclaves such as were found in midwestern and eastern industrial cities, nonetheless, various ethnic groups staked out social and cultural space, contributing to the city's cosmopolitan character.

Chinese men and women had lived in Sacramento since the gold rush days, the 1852 census showing 814 males and 10 females. Chinese workers increased in numbers when they were recruited to help build the Central Pacific. These early settlers were merchants, restaurateurs, laundrymen, peddlers, and providers of other services. Settling in on I Street and also near Sutter Slough (rechristened China Slough and China Lake), the Chinese enclave contained theaters, gambling houses, a local newspaper, and religious houses including not only family altars, but also a joss house and a Christian chapel run by the Congregationalists. Other Christian denominations also opened missions in the sometimes labeled Chinatown area and assisted the newcomers in learning English.

Distaste for the Chinese had always been in evidence in Sacramento, but it grew during the 1870s after the railroad work was completed. Popular presentations of the Chinese by the press derided the prevalence of Asian prostitution, the high incidence of gambling, and the existence of lotteries and opium dens. Legal efforts to exclude and restrict the Chinese began in the 1870s. In 1876, 4,000 Sacramentans, mostly members of the Sacramento Order of Caucasians, promoted white labor at an anti-Chinese meeting. In 1878, the Sacramento City Council sent a telegram to President Rutherford B. Hayes, urging him to sign legislation to limit Chinese immigration. The famous Workingman's Party, an offshoot of the anti-Chinese movement in San Francisco, led by Irish immigrant Denis Kearney, petitioned to have the Chinese excluded from municipal employment in Sacramento. In July 1879, Kearney himself appeared in Sacramento and, at a rally that drew nearly 3,000 people, raged against land monopoly and "consumptive politicians," specifically calling on them to "drive out the Chinese who are swarming all over the state of California." Although efforts by the Board of Trustees failed to exclude Chinese from the city, the anti-Chinese movement essentially achieved its goal when an 1882 Federal Exclusion Law, endorsed by California congressmen, barred future Chinese immigration. This law was extended for another ten years in 1892.

German-speaking Sacramentans, like the Chinese, had been present from the beginning of the city. The 1852 census identified 730 Germans in the county. By 1860, the number climbed to 1,634 and the number of German speakers (Germans, Swiss, and Austrians) peaked at 2,200 in the 1890s. German-speaking Sacramentans, although diverse in background, came to positions of prominence. One such figure was August Coolot, a local tobacconist (and early investor in the Central Pacific) whose reclusive ways belied a vast fortune. Others included his son-in-law Melchior Diepenbrock, the patriarch of a large and professionally prominent Sacramento family. Prominent Sacramentans of German background included Charles Matthias Goethe, a real estate speculator and eugenicist. Goethe had married into a large fortune and bestowed money liberally on pet causes, especially Sacramento State University. The Breuner family dominated the furniture industry; Joseph Hobrecht was well-known for his lighting fixtures, while Adolph Teichert raked in millions as an engineering contractor and aggregate tycoon. The community had its own newspaper, the *Nord California Herold* and maintained a spirit of cohesiveness focused around social organizations like the *Turnverein* (Turners), an athletic-social club that erected a large social hall. German life also focused around the German Evangelical Church, begun in 1867. In 1919, the congregation renamed itself St. John's Lutheran. St. John's welcomed a substantial number of well-to-do German-speaking families, and under the 40-year pastorate of Reverend Charles Oehler continued German language services until World War I. St. Francis of Assisi Catholic Church, although officially a multiethnic parish, also catered to German-speaking Catholics through the work of the Franciscan Friars of Teutopolis, Illinois.

Italians also joined Sacramento's working class in the nineteenth and twentieth centuries. Though only 41 Italians were registered in the 1852 census, the Italian contingent had risen to nearly 2,700 by 1910. According to historian Bruce Pierini, many Italians were recruited from eastern states and directly from Italy for the Southern Pacific Railyards. Census figures placed Italians as the third largest unskilled group working for the railroads in 1900. By 1910, they were the largest and held that place until 1924. Most of Sacramento's Italian colony were northern Italians, but the city also had a small cadre of Sicilians. Early Sacramento Italians also worked as cooks or in the business of lodge keeping. David DeBernardi ran the popular Sacramento Market. Italian Sacramentans enjoyed informal leadership from men like Luigi Caffaro, the owner of the Commercial Hotel, and had their own newspaper (*La Capitale*) under the editorship of Adriano Mazzini from 1907 until the 1940s. Most Sacramento Italians were Catholics, and in 1906

The first Breuner's store (established in 1856) was located at Sixth and K Streets.

the Diocese of Sacramento permitted the establishment of St. Mary's at Eighth and N, a national church. The church moved to Seventh and T Streets in 1914 and later relocated to the eastern end of the city at 58th and M after World War II. St. Mary's Italian priests played an important role in community formation through religious services, newspaper articles, and later radio broadcasts. One of the pastors of St. Mary's, Father Dominic Taverna, helped found the social/cultural Dante Club.

Sacramento was also a popular magnet for various groups of Portuguese. Several distinct groups of Portuguese-speaking immigrants made their way to Sacramento and its environs in the latter part of the nineteenth century. These included Portuguese from the continent as well as the more numerous Azoreans (others came from the Madeiras and Cape Verde Islands). As with most groups, the first Portuguese came with the gold rush. Many who came later first devoted themselves to agricultural pursuits across the river in Bryte and Broderick, on the south side of Sacramento, and in the Freeport/Clarksburg area. Others established successful businesses. Sacramento Portuguese arrayed themselves in a neighborhood south of R Street called "Arizona" (a corruption of the term Azores), and there built a small community that had as its center a Portuguese national church named for St. Elizabeth at 12th and S Streets (founded in 1912).

57

THE RAILROAD YARDS

The medley of ethnic groups that took up residence in Sacramento did so for railroad related work. The Central Pacific reached Promontory Summit in Utah on April 30, 1869 and was joined to the Union Pacific. The driving of the golden spike and the completion of the line on May 10, 1869 put Sacramento into the national transportation network and made the city a terminus for people, freight, mail, and locally grown produce headed for the tables of the East. The Central Pacific became the most important business in the state and absorbed other railroads, including the SVRR, as well as other transportation enterprises—river lines, stagecoaches, and cartage companies. It also absorbed a potential rival, the Southern Pacific (SP), a company whose name became the umbrella for the Big Four's vast transportation monopoly. Under SP were river boats, bay ferries, ocean liners, cable car lines, extensive real estate holdings, and timber and oil companies. SP became Sacramento's largest employer. Eventually the Big Four took up residence in more opulent San Francisco, but they left a growing work-force of engineers, laborers, shop workers, and administrators in Sacramento, most of whom worked in the repair and construction shops. The Goss & Lambard machine shop and foundry were the nucleus of the later sprawling railroad yards, which became one of the largest industrial sites in the western United States.

The shops grew steadily, with the city graciously ceding land the company required for expansion. In the shops, workers repaired rolling stock and produced an amazing array of products needed by the company: from office equipment to boilers and engines. From 1872 to 1937, some 272 engines rolled off the production lines. Shop craftsmen also made elaborate silver palace sleepers, water pumps, and even 100 of San Francisco's fabled cable cars. One of the first electric light plants on the Pacific Coast was designed and built in the shops. The presence of the yards brought stable work at good wages for the denizens of Sacramento. As the shops dominated the city's economy, so also did the railroad exercise significant influence over class status and politics in the city.

AGRICULTURE

The railroad also stimulated the development of valley agriculture, a mainstay of California's economy for many years. The rich soils of the Sacramento and San Joaquin Valleys produced needed grains and fruits that could now be marketed beyond the relatively small California market. The railroad gave impetus to the production of wheat, which could be easily shipped. The city had a number of mills. One of the most prominent was the Phoenix Mills, established in 1881. By 1894, the mill was running night and day, churning out 200 barrels of flour per day. The Pioneer Mills belonged to the milling giant, Sperry Flour Company, and had begun in 1856 with old-fashioned grinding stones activated by water from the American River. Indeed, Sacramento mills churned out thousands of barrels of flour until eventually business slowed in the wake of declining international prices and stiff competition from other parts of the country.

Crop lands in the county produced grapes near Rancho Cordova, pears, asparagus, and berries in the Delta, and oranges and other citrus fruits in Citrus Heights, Orangevale, and Fair Oaks. The invention of workable refrigerator cars in the 1880s made it possible to ship Central Valley fruits and vegetables long distances. Many of these fruits were shipped east in refrigerated cars cooled by huge blocks of ice from the high Sierras. By 1901, a huge ice house had been built in nearby Roseville that chilled fruits for shipments going east. Canning became another important Sacramento industry stimulated by the transcontinental railroad. Canning technology did not progress substantially until the time of the Civil War. However, by 1864, Sacramento had its first salmon cannery. J. Routier began the first fruit cannery in the Sacramento Valley in 1876. In 1882, the Capitol Packing Company on Front and K Streets was opened and by 1888 employed 450 people.

With the opening of the Panama Canal in 1914, the market for California canned goods increased dramatically and other regional canneries opened. Hunt Brothers began canning operations in Davis and Marysville. By 1912, Libby, McNeill & Libby had already opened a Sacramento facility that became one of California's largest. The California Packing Company and Bercut Richards also built huge facilities. Some growers and shippers reacted to the increasing consolidation of the packing industry by forming cooperatives, associations, and exchanges. Sacramento's most famous example of this is the California Almond

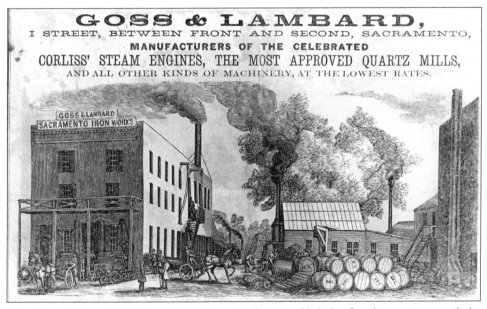

The Goss & Lambard Sacramento Iron Works assembled the first locomotives until the Central Pacific Railroad built their own shops, which became the nucleus of the expansive Southern Pacific rail yards.

By 1894, the Phoenix Milling Company ran day and night, churning out 200 barrels of flour per day.

Growers Exchange, which still ships tons of locally produced almonds around the world. The seasonal work patterns of the canneries also set a tone for the working-class culture of Sacramento. Canneries provided an opportunity for immigrant women to develop work skills and add to their family's income. The net result of this increasingly diverse workforce was a slow but steady increase in Sacramento's population. In 1860, 13,875 people resided in the city. By 1900, nearly 30,000 called Sacramento home.

RAILROAD DOMINANCE OF SACRAMENTO POLITICS

The economic dominance of the railroad extended to other aspects of the city's development. Sacramento was a microcosm of the advantages and liabilities of American industrialization. Industrial work and wages brought wealth, stability, and the prospect of serious urban building. It also brought pollution, periodic depression, the absorption of prime city lands, and the undemocratic manipulation of city politics.

The railroad hooked Sacramento on its jobs and occasionally played the city like a flute when it needed additional land and space for shop expansion. One such incident occurred in 1875 when company officials wanted to take over the old city waterworks property at I and Sixth Streets and demanded a portion of the riverfront to transform it into a rolling mill. Summoning city officials to their offices in San Francisco in February, the company promised to build the mill and assured the city fathers that this would bring even greater stability to the city. Recalling a similar incident two years earlier when railroad officials had insisted on representation on the city board of trustees in exchange for keeping the shops in the city, the editors of the *Sacramento Union* denounced the land grab and the company's efforts to subvert democracy. *Union* opposition displeased the railroad leadership, who began dropping dark hints about relocating the railroad yards to Oakland. Local citizens, fearful of angering the city's chief employer, reacted immediately and organized a mass meeting of nearly 600 people at Turner Hall. Those attending heard the report of a meeting with Leland Stanford and another committee at which the company had assured them of its willingness to stay in Sacramento. But the railroad made no bones about its desire to control the city: they asked that in local elections no one be nominated to an elected city office who was hostile to the railroad. Those assembled at Turner Hall capitulated to railroad demands and, through a series of propositions, declared "that it is manifestly for the best interests of the city to cultivate friendly relations with the Directors of the Central Pacific Company."

When the headstrong *Union* kept up a sarcastic barrage against the company, decrying those who were "bringing Sacramento in chains before Leland Stanford," its days were numbered. By the end of February 1875, the offending *Union* had been purchased by the railroad's organ, the rival *Sacramento Record*. The *Record-Union* soon squashed any critical spirit and lauded the economic development of Sacramento, counting the railroad yards as the city's main hope for a bright future.

From the 1870s on, the railroad exercised considerable control over local politics, to the extent that their political operatives directed the voting patterns of the yard workers. Railroad agents became increasingly adept at working with local politicians of both parties. Company "bosses," like gambler Frank Rhodes and hops-grower Bartley Cavanaugh (father of a later city manager), picked candidates for city trustee as well as state and federal office. William F. Herrin, head of the Southern Pacific political bureau, conveyed railroad wishes to local politicians and plied officials with free passes on the rail lines. Though technically illegal under the State Constitution of 1879, this standard bribe continued for many years. Herrin resided part-time in Sacramento and gave Bartley Cavanaugh's address as his residence.

Class Struggle

Once the basic parameters of railroad control were established, the relationship between city and railroad was usually peaceful. A series of competent superintendents oversaw the needs of the railroad workers, perhaps the most legendary being Andrew Jackson Stevens, memorialized by a bronze statue in present-day Cesar Chavez Park. Stevens was master mechanic of the shops and the one responsible for introducing the construction of locomotives to the

Sacramento yards. Stevens practiced a form of paternalism, refusing to lay off workers during tough times, choosing instead to reduce hours and declining to keep a "black list" of those fired. When he died in 1888, the workers collected nearly $5,300 for the statue.

Even though men like Stevens demonstrated a benign paternalism, others did not feel positively inclined toward the railroad. There were those who felt short-changed by the inability of the industrial world to distribute wealth equitably or to offer respite from monopolistic or heavy-handed actions by industrial leaders who manipulated government and other public institutions to serve their own ends. In California, farmers disgruntled with the practices and rates of Southern Pacific spearheaded the first reactions against big business. In 1878, a branch of the national farmer's organization, the Grange, was organized in Sacramento. As farmer discontent spread to more organizations, Sacramento found itself receptive to an early coherent voice of disgruntlement: the Populist Party.

The emergence of Populism in the 1890s reflected a widespread discontent in the nation's agricultural areas and drew strong support in Sacramento. In fact, the reformist agenda of the Populists in 1896 caused the *Daily Bee*, by then edited by the son of James McClatchy, Charles Kenny McClatchy, to turn from its traditional backing of Republican candidates and to throw support behind the Democratic/Populist nominee, William Jennings Bryan. Charles Kenny McClatchy, known as C.K., had taken over the editorial writing at the paper after the death of his father in 1883. C.K., like his father, would become a powerful voice for reform in the city. Ruggedly independent, he withdrew somewhat from his strong support of local Populist politicians when many of them became involved in the anti-Catholic American Protective Association (APA), which attempted to exclude Catholics from public office. The association of reformers with the APA undercut their agenda for a time.

THE PULLMAN STRIKE: LABOR VIOLENCE

The presence of the railroad also played a critical role in one of the major labor disruptions of nineteenth-century America, the Pullman Strike of 1894. The rise of organized labor was slow in Sacramento. Historian Carson Sheetz noted that from the 1850s through the 1880s, assorted strike actions punctuated various labor venues (cartage, teamsters, and construction) and that various groups of workers pushed for the eight-hour workday. However, Sacramento's only recognized labor organization was the Typographical Union, a fairly moribund association chartered in November 1859. Working-class issues quickened with the activity of the Workingman's Party in the 1870s. Labor issues usually centered on the desire to drive out the "cheap labor" of the Chinese. One of Sacramento's early labor leaders was a young carpenter, J.D. Jost, who was at the center of whatever labor organizing activities took place from the 1870s through the 1890s. Jost was a highly respected figure and won general acceptance by avoiding inflammatory and class-based rhetoric. The advent of the national Knights of

Young Sacramento Bee *editor*
Charles Kenny (C.K.) McClatchy
became a powerful voice for reform in
the city.

Labor in the last decades of the nineteenth century stirred some interest in Sacramento, but there was no enthusiasm for an organization that combined skilled and unskilled laborers, the hallmark of the Knight's membership.

The turning point for local labor came when Sacramento experienced a population and housing boom in the 1880s. Spurred partly by competition with rapidly growing Los Angeles, Sacramento began to lay out more areas for development, building more homes, more public transportation, and other urban infrastructure. The increasing demands for labor created a temporary labor shortage in Sacramento and skilled workers from a variety of trades picked up the pace of labor association. In August 1889, a Sacramento Federated Trades Council was formed, comprised of 11 skilled local trade unions. The numbers soon grew.

Sacramento's reputation for fairly amicable labor relations hit bumps throughout its history. A strike (endorsed by the Trades Council), by the typographers at the *Bee* in late 1890 and early 1891, nearly brought the paper to its knees. But the worst flare-up of labor unrest took place in the midst of a national depression and the 1894 Pullman Strike.

On May 1, 1894, workers at the Pullman Yards, a railroad car manufacturing site near Chicago, went on strike, protesting reduced wages and benefits. They refused to couple Pullman cars, and they blocked trains that carried the offensive cars. The Pullman workers were not unionized at the time, but socialist leader Eugene V. Debs, head of the United Railway Workers, helped the workers press their cause.

Strikers during the Pullman Strike sabotage a train on the Yolo trestle, 3 miles west of Sacramento, July 11, 1894.

Around the nation, the prospect of rail turmoil sent shock waves through a country now heavily dependent on regular rail traffic. The standoff between workers and the company resulted in a federal injunction against the workers, who responded with acts of violence and destruction of cars. The strike found sympathetic supporters in the American West, especially in rail centers like San Francisco, Oakland, and Sacramento. In June 1894, workers at the Southern Pacific yards declared solidarity with their fellow laborers in Illinois and declared a secondary boycott, refusing to move any train with a Pullman car. Southern Pacific retaliated by closing the freight operations, and eventually all work in the yards stopped.

Workers then took over the yards and stations. Despite Southern Pacific demands that strikers be arrested, city officials resisted. Efforts to calm the situation were ignored and eventually federal marshals were sent in to end the boycott. When an impasse was reached, the U.S. marshal called on the governor for three regiments of the local National Guard. In a tense standoff on the Fourth of July 1894, nearly 1,000 guardsmen confronted strikers. When they were ordered to fix bayonets and march on the strikers, many of whom were friends and neighbors, the Guard refused and withdrew. Federal intervention came next. On July 10, President Cleveland ordered the strikers to stand down or be arrested. When shots were exchanged, federal troops arrived on July 11 from the San Francisco Presidio, and U.S. Marines and Army cavalry secured the Sacramento depot and rail yards. In retaliation, local radicals wrecked a train on the Yolo Bypass, killing several soldiers and rail workers. Labor peace eventually returned, but a number of the strikers were blackballed by a vengeful company.

BUILDING THE CITY: ELECTRICITY AND TRANSPORTATION

The development of urban infrastructure continued apace. By 1854, a city hall had been constructed. The creation of a stable city water supply had been an item on the public agenda since the disastrous fires of the early 1850s. In 1852, city residents approved a tax increase to pay for a new waterworks and it was completed in April 1854. However, the production of a clean, reliable water supply would continue to vex Sacramento for many years. City drinking water contained visible sediment derisively called "Sacramento Straight," and disagreements over the best method of providing clean water prevented a comprehensive city-wide approach until voters approved bonds for a new water filtration plant in the 1920s.

The city's sewer system also required continual updating. The first Sacramento sewers were put in place in 1853. This primitive water disposal system was only designed to handle the excess of rain water and not the increasing amount of human waste deposited by the growing population. Citizens dumped their personal waste and their used bath and laundry water into backyard privies and the China Slough for many years. Outdoor privies were the rule in most homes—literally a trench behind the home. Water closets made their first appearance in Sacramento in 1870 and were soon integrated into the design of public buildings like the County Hospital and large city hotels and eventually private homes. Garbage collection was improved in 1895 when the city hired a private scavenger. In 1922, the city assumed the responsibility. For many years, city garbage was incinerated.

In 1855, gas mains began to be laid down the main streets, illuminating Sacramento's nighttime darkness. Telegraph transmission had been the city's first form of instant communication, and after Alexander Graham Bell had successfully demonstrated the telephone at the 1876 Centennial Exposition in Philadelphia, Sacramentans, like other Americans, soon developed a fascination with the talking box. In 1878, the first two phones in Sacramento connected the Carriage Manufacture Company and the Music Parlor. Later, the phone was hooked up to the telegraph lines and communication with San Francisco commenced. Sacramento's first continuous phone line was begun in 1879—a 5-mile long circuit that connected 29 businesses with a central exchange. The Western Union office served as the first informal telephone exchange, with lines strung from homes and businesses to the telegraph office. In 1880, the Sacramento Telephonic Exchange began and was then purchased by the Bell Company. A rival company originated in 1895 that for a time created confusion since calls could not be patched through from one company to another. These two companies merged in 1902, and in 1906 renamed themselves the Pacific Telephone & Telegraph Company.

Sacramentans gradually embraced electricity as their main power source. Privately owned steam generators had powered the first electric lights in Sacramento as early as 1879, when the *Sacramento Union* and the Weinstock,

Lubin & Co. department store co-sponsored a magnificent display of electric lighting during State Fair week. The newspaper generated the energy from its steam presses, and it was carried over wires on rooftops to a set of arc lights in store display windows.

In the 1880s, a number of hydraulic mining companies tested the possibility of hydroelectric power in the Mother Lode. The leaders of the Natoma Water and Mining Company—Horatio Gates Livermore along with his sons and Albert Gallatin, a manager of the Huntington/Hopkins Hardware Store—secured enough capital to build a small dam and powerhouse on the American River at Folsom. On July 13, 1895, Sacramentans were awakened at 4 a.m. to the sound of a 100-gun salute announcing that electrical power was pulsing 22 miles from Folsom into the state capital, at the time the longest electrical transmission in the world and the second in the United States. On September 9, Admission Day, Sacramento hosted a spectacular electrical parade to celebrate the coming of electricity to the capital city. Over 60,000 witnessed the spectacle, which included 25,000 colored lights wrapped around poles and the illumination of the state capitol building. By 1899, the demand for power had escalated to the point that a second power station was created on the North Fork of the Yuba River. Sacramento soon became fully electric, with street lights, neon signs, and streetcars powered by the alternating current generated by the same mountain streams that had once threatened doom for the city.

Electricity also provided a power source for urban transportation and for the spatial expansion of the city. The city's road paving technology evolved from dirt paths to the simple plank roads that had paved the way to the gold fields to later roads paved with macadamized stone. With the advent of public transportation by streetcars, roads that had long been dirt and dust now needed hard surfaces to accommodate the heavy streetcars zigzagging down the main business districts and out to the residential areas. Beginning in 1858, horse drawn carriages conveyed passengers from Third and R to the commercial district at Second and K. In 1861, car tracks were laid on city streets to facilitate transport systems. In 1890, the Livermores incorporated the Sacramento Electric Power & Light Company and obtained a franchise from the city to build an electric streetcar system, and by 1895, this system was tied to the hydroelectric power that flowed in Sacramento. In 1906, Pacific Gas & Electric (PG & E) took over the system and controlled the supply of electricity and gas for years. From the company's car barns at 28th and N Streets ran 11 lines that crisscrossed the city. The shops of the company also built a number of streetcars. This public transit system dominated Sacramento until the 1940s when it was replaced by buses and automobiles.

Streetcars meant spatial expansion and a greater distinction between residential and working centers. As the old horse-drawn cars were transformed to the new electrical cars, a sorting out of urban space soon segregated the "homes" (east of 16th Street) from the business and commercial district—and also from the older housing stock of the West End that would soon be predominately occupied by the foreign-born and the working class.

Hydroelectric power came to Sacramento, lighting up the capitol building in September 1895.

PROMOTING THE CITY: CREATING URBAN LEGENDS

A new generation of Sacramentans emerged to lead the city into the new century. Earlier community leaders like Hopkins, Huntington, Stanford, and Crocker had stepped forward to meet the challenges of a changing city life. But in 1873, they moved the headquarters of the Central Pacific out of Sacramento (and themselves with it) and took up residence in San Francisco. The departure of this wealthy cadre (a not uncommon occurrence with Sacramentans who had made their fortunes) gave the city something of a collective inferiority complex. However, a new generation of leaders surfaced, led by Albert Gallatin and local businessman Joseph Steffens. In 1873, a Board of Trade was formed to promote business interests. Steffens, Gallatin, and Sacramento mayor Christopher Green formed part of this group dedicated to creating a better climate for urban development.

The 1870s were a time of financial stress and difficulty for Sacramento as promised railroad wealth did not immediately materialize. However, in the 1880s, a land boom, spurred in part by aggressive railroad advertising in the East, began to bring more people to California. When the majority of these newcomers moved to Southern California, Sacramento developers scrambled to seek their share of the settlers. To compete with the allure of citrus fruits promoted by Southern California advertisers, Sacramento merchants began their own fruit colonies in the eastern part of the county in communities like Orangevale and Fair

Oaks. These two small villages were actively marketed as places of health and sunshine, able to produce a superior breed of orange, grapefruit, and lemon. The McClatchy brothers at the *Bee* joined in the effort to move Sacramento in a new direction. Both brothers railed incessantly against anything or anybody that stood in the way. Relentlessly they pressed Sacramento to improve its water supply, pave its roads, clean up its politics, eliminate its vice and crime, and beautify its streets by planting trees. In 1894, the *Bee* issued a huge promotional tract, *Where California Fruits Grow: A Resource of Sacramento County*. Written in the "high booster" style of nineteenth-century city "boomers" and lavishly illustrated, the publication was distributed far and wide to lure people to the city. Goaded by the increasing demand for more organization and planning in city development, in 1895, a new Chamber of Commerce succeeded the somewhat informal Board of Trade and became even more focused on marketing Sacramento.

Historical memory was also drafted in the quest to create a new, improved Sacramento. One group that contributed mightily to the creation of a historic past for Sacramento was the Sacramento Pioneers. This organization of citizens who had been residents of California before 1850 was founded in 1854. The initial group consisted of 70 male citizens who still had first-hand memories of early Sacramento. The group devoted itself to collecting books and memorabilia of the city's past and eventually built a hall to store them. Pioneer Hall at 1009 Seventh Street hosted meetings and public events. Pioneer Society members, especially James McClatchy, spoke often at public gatherings, evoking the spirit of Sacramento's past. Annual celebrations of the Fourth of July became an important moment for Pioneer speakers to recall their memories for a new generation as they were often asked to give the formal address for the day. As time went on, these memories took on a warmer and more romantic glow—and in some cases were so embellished as to bear little resemblance to the truth. Nonetheless, like most cities, Sacramento developed its core of urban myths that helped define its identity and could also be used to attract others to the city. Books, such as Thompson and West's 1888 compendium of Sacramento life and history, included lithographs of city residences and also biographies of leading citizens wealthy enough to purchase a space in the tome.

The Pioneers left their mark on Sacramento through their efforts to reclaim a decrepit Sutter's Fort. By 1895, the fort was nearly a complete ruin. When it was proposed to run the city streetcar system through the property, the Sacramento Pioneers mobilized to save this remnant of Sacramento's past. They forged an alliance with a new group, the Native Sons and Daughters of the Golden West, purchased the property, and began to rehabilitate it. Later, the State of California finished the job and it became a state park. These nostalgic groups did much to market the legend of John Sutter as the "founder" of Sacramento—a myth that passed into the textbooks printed by the State of California and was mandated as part of the statewide curriculum for students in elementary schools.

Historical memories played an important role in the creation of promotional materials for the city. Pamphlets, brochures, posters, and other materials constantly stressed Sacramento's gold rush past and down-played memories of the early struggles of the city: fires, floods, and epidemics (except to note the heroism of the people in combating them). Sacramento's benign climate, its economic vitality, its cultural institutions, schools, health care facilities, the elegance of its buildings (especially the state capitol and the nearby Catholic Cathedral of the Blessed Sacrament), as well as its entrepreneurial drive were promoted in order to bring more people to live in Sacramento.

Architectural and Cultural Enhancements

With stability and wealth enough, Sacramento began to look more and more like a city. In 1872, a retrospective by the *Sacramento Union* lauded the city's growth made possible by "her mechanics" and the "new industries." Public schools were enlarged, the seat of government had been finished, the Odd Fellows had erected a new temple, and Sacramentans looked forward to a permanent governor's mansion. Local developers like Joseph Steffens pressed hard for river improvements and encouraged vigorous city promotion. At Steffens's urging, Sacramento won federal funds in 1887 for a new federal building at Seventh and K that included a postal facility to handle the increasing volume of mail and business coming into Sacramento. This handsome sandstone structure resembled a castle and remained on the site until it was torn down in the 1950s. Churches

Pioneer Hall, here decorated for a parade to honor President Benjamin Harrison's visit on May 2, 1891, hosted meetings and events.

69

also played an important role, not only in the maturation of city life but also in providing buildings of exceptional elegance.

Roman Catholics were the first to make Sacramento a regional church headquarters. Irish immigrant Bishop Patrick Manogue transferred the center of operations of the Catholic Church of Northern California from Grass Valley to Sacramento in 1886. Soon after, he commenced the building of a new Roman Catholic cathedral based on the design of the Parisian church of the Holy Trinity. Set deliberately at 11th and K, one block north of the capitol, it was intended to complement the state house. In May 1886, workmen began digging the foundation of the Cathedral of the Blessed Sacrament. The mammoth new church was dedicated in solemn rites held at the end of June 1889.

In 1899, the Episcopal Church made Sacramento the headquarters of a Missionary District under the leadership of Bishop William Hall Moreland. Between 1903 and 1908, the Episcopalians built the handsome neo-Gothic St. Paul Church on the corner of 15th and K. A small chapel named for St. Andrew was moved from 23rd and K to 26th and M Streets. Later, a bishop's residence and the Episcopal Trinity Cathedral were erected on this site.

Sacramento in this period began to develop as a mature city. In the 1880s and 1890s, developing city neighborhoods began to showcase elegant Victorian homes, especially along H Street. Perhaps the most elegant was hardware merchant Albert Gallatin's magnificent residence on the corner of 16th and H. Later sold to Joseph Steffens (father of future muckraker Lincoln Steffens), the

The Cathedral of the Blessed Sacrament, based on the design of the Parisian Church of the Holy Trinity, was the second highest building in Sacramento, second only to the state capitol, in 1889.

home embodied many of the finest features of Sacramento's Victorians with gilded ceilings, hardwood floors, and odd shaped rooms. In 1903, it became the governor's mansion (previously California governors had lived in hotels or private homes). Governor George Pardee became its first full-time resident and subsequent governors lived there until 1967 when California First Lady Nancy Reagan refused to live in the "old fire trap." It is now a state museum.

Social and cultural life quickened as well. In 1884, a coterie of Sacramentans led by merchant David Lubin formed the California Museum Association "to foster art, science, mechanics and literature" in Sacramento. The association brokered the transfer to the city of a private gallery attached to the estate of E.B. and Margaret Crocker on Third and O Streets. The residence had been the former home of merchant B.F. Hastings and was sold to Judge E.B. Crocker (brother of Big Four magnate Charles Crocker) and his wife Margaret. Local architect Seth Babson renovated, expanded, embellished, and remade it into an Italianate mansion for the Crockers. Behind the home, Babson constructed a gallery that incorporated bowling alleys, a skating rink, and a billiards room. The gallery was intended to house an eclectic art collection that the Crockers had accumulated in their various travels abroad. This collection included 1,000 drawings and other works by contemporary California artists. In 1885, Margaret Crocker deeded the gallery to the city and the Museum Association organized displays of its various objects. Thousands of grateful Sacramentans attended a Flower Festival held in honor of "Lady Bountiful" in May 1885. Her later benefactions included the donation of imported windows to the Catholic Cathedral of the Blessed Sacrament and to St. Paul's Episcopal Church. Sadly, her affection for the city evaporated in 1891 when a lawsuit against a German maid accused of stealing from Crocker's daughter Aimee declared the defendant innocent—despite Margaret's corroborating testimony. Angered that her word in favor of her daughter had not been accepted by a Sacramento court, she quit Sacramento in 1892 and moved to New York, where she died in 1901.

Her late pique at the city notwithstanding, she was one of its greatest benefactors. Even before she donated the gallery, in 1882 she had purchased and expanded a large house, known as the Marguerite Home, at Seventh and Q Streets as a shelter for older women lacking visible means of support. In 1884, she purchased two square blocks across from the City Cemetery on Broadway and built a $40,000 botanical garden. In 1901, Margaret Crocker signed over her mansion to the Peniel Rescue Mission for the care of "erring young women." Margaret's daughter Jennie later repurchased the former family home and it, along with the attached gallery, became the West's first public art museum. Crocker's generosity was matched by Jane Stanford, wife of the governor, who donated art works to local churches and her own home to the Sisters of Mercy for an orphanage.

Since few others in Sacramento had the wealth of the Crockers or the Stanfords, charitable individuals formed private associations, mostly comprised of Sacramento women, who cared for the city's poor. For example, an association of women who founded the Protestant Orphan Asylum took up the care of orphan children.

HEALTH CARE

Sacramento's early health care history paralleled the development of the field of medicine. From gold rush days on, Sacramento had a cadre of doctors who helped to care for the needs of the sick. Hospital care, which in the early nineteenth century did not have a strong therapeutic thrust, also existed in the city. One of the first city hospitals was in an adobe building at Sutter's Fort. A medley of private hospitals were created around the city. Sacramento County opened its public hospital in 1853 at the corner of I and Seventh Streets, moving it in 1867 to L Street between Tenth and 11th (the capitol grounds today). In 1870, the county purchased 60 acres on Upper Stockton Road where over the years they have enlarged and modernized the public hospital. Important doctors in Sacramento's health care history include Dr. John Frederick Morse, also noted as one of the city's first historians. Dr. J.D.T. Stillman worked with Morse to create a respectable health care presence in Sacramento, and Dr. Gregory Phelan, a New York doctor, played an important role in shaping policies related to public health as well as public education. The advent of the railroad shops and the significant number of job-related injuries caused the railroad to open The Central Pacific Hospital in November 1868. Providing an employer-subsidized medical service for injured workers, it collected dues from the workers and employed a number of city physicians who tended to injured or ill workers at the hospital and at home.

Early Sacramento doctors were a mix of professionally trained and self-proclaimed physicians. After several false starts, the city formed the Sacramento Society for Medical Improvement in 1868. Leading this association of physicians was Dr. Gustavus Simmons, who attempted to professionalize the health care field and opened the Ridge Home Sanitarium in the 1880s. The home was a combination of nursing home and operating hospital, but clearly not the kind of specialized institution that would be recognized as a hospital today. Eventually, Simmons and other city physicians cajoled the Sisters of Mercy to take over the project, which they did in 1895, creating Mater Misericordiae Hospital, known popularly as Sisters Hospital. The sisters re-did the hodge-podge of buildings and wards and created a unified institution that resembled more clearly a hospital. However, the city was slow to respond to public health issues, and some believe that the prevalence of contagious illnesses in Sacramento slowed its growth.

THE LEGACY OF DAVID LUBIN

Sacramento's adoption of consumerism as a way of life took hold gradually as the downtown began to arrange itself into a new commercial district. Popular emporia or department stores led the way. In 1874, David Lubin opened the Mechanics Store, a dry goods business on the southeast corner of K and Fourth Streets. The store introduced an innovation in Sacramento retailing by operating on a cash-only basis and insisting on fixed prices for its goods. He was joined by his half-brother, Harris Weinstock, and the store was renamed Weinstock, Lubin

& Company in imitation of eastern emporia that used family names. As business picked up, Weinstock and Lubin added on to their store, which eventually engulfed most of the block. Once his fortune was made, the intense Lubin turned to public affairs and played a key role in the development of Sacramento cultural life. In 1901, he wrote a philosophical treatise entitled *Let There Be Light* and devoted the rest of his life to the issue of balancing agricultural supply with world demand for food. In 1905, with the blessing of the Italian royal family, he opened the International Institute of Agriculture in Rome, with 46 nations participating. Lubin died in Rome on New Year's Day 1919 and is memorialized in the name of a Sacramento grade school and a street in the Eternal City, Viale Lubin at the edge of the Villa Borghese. In 1946, the United Nations Food and Agriculture Organization absorbed the work he began.

The railroad helped define a new era in Sacramento and the forces of development helped the city create a more visible and settled atmosphere. Sacramento did not grow rapidly during this time, hampered in part by disease, slow development of its roads, transportation system, and other appurtenances of urban living. However, the twinkling lights of the electric parade, the successful effort to stave off capital removal, and the formation of a new and even more aggressive development association, the Chamber of Commerce, provided yet another moment when *Urbs Indomita* asserted itself.

Merchant and philanthropist David Lubin, shown here c. 1913, devoted the latter part of his life to agricultural issues and the world demand for food.

4. RETOOLING FOR MODERN TIMES

Igniting the fires of reform in late nineteenth-century Sacramento was not easy. For nearly ten years, C.K. McClatchy of the *Bee* had derided the city administration and the pace of urban improvement as "Silurian"—a typical McClatchy neologism for backwards. Others shared the editor's dim view of Sacramento's poor streets, brackish water, and undeveloped cultural and social life. State legislators in particular bridled against staying too long in the heat and smell and disease of Sacramento for the infrequent sessions of the state legislature. State offices scattered to more pleasant locations. Legislators particularly resented the hypercritical tone of the *Bee*. Smouldering discontent among the solons over sessions in "dull" Sacramento was ignited by McClatchy's needling in March 1893 when the *Bee* sarcastically "celebrated" the end of a legislative session with a bold headline begun "Thank God." Angry legislators denounced the newspaper and in retaliation introduced a bill to remove the capital from Sacramento. Fortunately, the efforts faltered (as did another attempt spearheaded by a vengeful Southern Pacific early in the twentieth century). But the very possibility that state government might pull out of Sacramento galvanized city leaders to take action and mobilize a cadre of middle-class reformers who insisted on a cleaner and more efficient Sacramento. McClatchy later claimed credit for bringing Sacramento out of its "Silurian" period. But the editor's self-promotion notwithstanding, Sacramento did embark on an important period of physical and social transformation in the late nineteenth and early twentieth centuries. At the same time the restoration of national prosperity in the latter half of the 1890s and energetic local leadership stimulated by the national and state Progressive movements gave Sacramento a new lease on life.

GOVERNMENT REFORM

The cumulative impact of industrial expansion and population growth presented new challenges. The development of electrical power, the internal combustion engine, the increasing popularity of secondary education, and the respect tendered to "scientific thinking" encouraged a local movement for efficiency and democracy. City government felt the first pressures of the new civic mood. The first city charter, forged in the 1850s, had provided for an elected mayor and a common council derived from the geographical boundaries of city wards. In 1857, the city and county governments merged for a time, an arrangement that lasted only until 1863. Urban-rural clashes doomed the alliance, and the city and county governments uncoupled when a new charter was drafted. The charter of 1863, which would be in place for more than 30 years, provided for three trustees elected by the voters at large. Each trustee took care of an aspect of city life: roads, public health, fire and police, etc.

As the city grew in size and complexity, the charter of 1863 became inadequate. Historian William Mahan has described the growing discontent with the existing system, which resulted in the 1893 revision. The process began when the city elected 15 freeholders, charged with the task of writing the new charter, in December 1891. The freeholders were a mix of some of the city's pioneers, like Judge J. Wesley Armstrong (who had come during the gold rush), along with new city leaders, including department store mogul Harris Weinstock, attorneys Robert Devlin and Grove Johnson, and future mayor Clinton White. The group completed their work by March 1892. The new charter created an independent mayor who ran the city like the executive of a company. An expanded board of trustees, which functioned as a legislative branch, complemented the newly empowered mayor. The city was divided into nine wards, with each ward electing its own trustee and its own representative on the board of education. The new document gave the mayor the right to appoint a number of officers with the consent of the Board of Trustees, including the chief of police, all 15 police

Sacramento lawyer and legislator Grove L. Johnson, shown here in 1906, was one of 15 freeholders elected in 1891 to write a new city charter.

75

officers, the city surveyor, superintendent of streets, fire chief and firemen, directors of cemeteries, and employees of the waterworks.

THE NEW URBAN POLITICS: RAILROAD CONTROL

The charter of 1893 created a more effective government to deal with issues plaguing Sacramento. Anxious city development types were eager to improve Sacramento's image and enhance its suitability for newcomers.

Public health issues continued to dog the city. Ineffective means of rodent extermination and foul-tasting drinking water continued to be problems, and city denizens refused to pass the tax bonds necessary to remedy these problems. Street cleaning, especially for the animal ordure left daily, was limited. Sacramento stunk, especially in the hot summer months. In addition to the waste left by animals on the streets, the city had seven dairies and several breweries within its limits, a foul smelling glue factory at 30th and U, as well as hog and cattle yards. Arguments over the surfacing of city streets raged continually. Some roads had been surfaced; others were still gravel and hardened soil, dusty in summer and mud pots in the rainy season. City vice, long a *bête noire* of respectable citizens and the object of erstwhile crusades by the newspapers, flourished. Prostitution was carried on in houses with the distinctive "1/2" on their addresses. Saloons, gambling, illegal lotteries, opium dens, and bars that stayed open all night were as hard to erase as original sin—and all of this vice appeared to go on under the noses (and perhaps with the tacit support) of the city administration and the police force.

Sacramento's poor streets were a source of complaint, as in this view of yet to be paved J Street looking west from about Seventh Street, 1868.

For some city officials, the time was ripe for a renegotiation of city dealings with the powerful railroad. The railroad's political control was obvious, and wily railroad political agents were still able to work with the new city administrations and especially the city council. However, city reformers soon began to identify the railroad with everything that kept Sacramento from urban greatness. The railroad, once hailed as the city's salvation, was increasingly viewed as a detriment to urban improvement. Donning the mantle of urban reformers, local progressives in Sacramento framed virtually every public issue as a struggle between the forces of urban advance and a reactionary cabal consisting of the overly powerful railroad, its puppet politicians, and immigrants. In fact, the division of the city into geographic wards by the charter made it easier to pit one group against another and accentuated class and socioeconomic differences as never before. Naturally, the poorer and more immigrant-heavy wards were targeted by reformers as sources of urban corruption while the more prosperous, upscale, Americanized wards were the sources of civic renewal. William Mahan relates that the "worst case" wards (as far as reformers were concerned) were the four in the city's West End, an area that took in the now decaying waterfront and the rail yards. The city's fifth ward was a swing ward, while wards six through nine were in newer residential districts—an area referred to as the "homes." Representing the poorer, working-class wards was the local Democratic Party. In this broad Democratic coalition were also the city's immigrant communities. These too were viewed suspiciously by reformers.

A More Diverse City

Among the growing number of nationalities clustered in the West End were Italians, Portuguese, Japanese, Croatians, and Filipinos. Japanese immigration to America began in the late nineteenth century. Most Japanese migrated to the West Coast, and thanks largely to the dynamic of chain-migration, Sacramento became one of the major cities for Japanese settlement. By 1900, there were 336 in the city and 1,209 in the county. By 1910, the numbers had escalated to nearly 1,500 and 3,874 respectively. Sacramentans awoke to the visibility of Japanese residents when nearly 700 gathered in McKinley Park in 1895 to celebrate the victory of their nation over China. Scattered Japanese agricultural settlements dotted the county, and in the city the Japanese Quarter (Japantown) was one of the larger ethnic enclaves stretching east from Second to Fifth Streets and south from L to O (the heart was between Third and Fourth and L and M). By 1911, historian Wayne Maeda notes that Sacramento's Japantown was self-contained and self-sufficient, with over 200 Japanese-owned businesses. The community had its own barber shops, pool halls, banks, hospitals, mutual aid societies, and an array of churches—Buddhist, Methodist, Presbyterian, and Baptist.

Joining the ethnic medley were also immigrants from the Balkans, largely Croats but also some Serbs. By 1930, there were nearly 1,000 of the first generation, many of whom worked in mining, railroading, farming, and canning.

The center of Croatian culture was the Rosemont Grill, where newly arrived Croatians found assistance and an informal labor exchange. Filipinos also joined the mix, and though few initially, large numbers began coming through Hawaii in 1898. The mix also included some Koreans and Punjabis as well.

Although the railroad worked well with both parties, Sacramento immigrants gravitated to the Democrats. The diverse Democratic coalition was held together by one of Sacramento's most skilled politicians, Thomas Fox, a native of Oak Park who was a career executive with the Pacific Mutual Life Insurance Company. Fox, twice postmaster of Sacramento under Democratic administrations, was a popular and effective politician. Edward J. Carraghar, who owned the popular Saddle Rock Restaurant on Second Street, assisted him. Southern Pacific political bureau director William F. Herrin used the time-honored "boss" system to continue to bend public policy to support railroad interests. Sacramento reformers took a dim view of railroad-oriented politics with its hint of corruption, based on transient and immigrant voters whom they believed were too easily manipulated by politicians and railroad company masters. City reformers were determined to end the dominance of what novelist Frank Norris referred to as the "Octopus."

PROGRESSIVE HIGH TIDE: THE WESTERN PACIFIC AND CLINTON F. WHITE

Sacramento's progressive reformers built on old Populist ideas and energy. New political leaders who disregarded and rejected old parties came on the scene and began to press a reform agenda. Interestingly, reform began with old-line politicians. Even though he was a "tool" of the Southern Pacific, Mayor William Land (1898–1899) and his successor George Clark (1900–1903), a local mortician, fought a successful battle to end illegal gambling at Sacramento's poolrooms. Victories piled up. In 1903, initiative and referendum were added to the city charter. Using the initiative helped end ward politics by mandating the election of each trustee at-large rather than by ward, making it possible for middle-class Sacramentans to outvote the working-class immigrant wards.

Sacramento women also contributed to the climate of reform by mobilizing to eliminate the influence of urban vice in the form of gambling halls and taverns. They provided critical support to the efforts of Mayors Land and Clark to end poolroom gambling. Linked to these efforts to eliminate sin was the cause of women's suffrage. Early efforts promoting women's suffrage began in 1871 when Mrs. L.G. Waterhouse, a midwife, "hydropathic" physician, and leader of the Sacramento Women's Suffrage Association, hosted veteran women's rights activist Susan B. Anthony for a rousing talk. Nonetheless, efforts by local women to move the state legislature to debate the matter waxed and waned until 1911 when it was put before the entire state in a referendum. By that time, the support of both papers, *Bee* and *Union*, was strong, and after a tense election day the state voted to grant women the vote. In August 1920, the rest of the country followed California's example and the 19th Amendment guaranteed women's suffrage.

The Western Pacific passenger depot in Sacramento was approved in spite of interference by Southern Pacific operatives.

The vote of women allowed middle-class voters to outnumber the transient-immigrant votes, which were exclusively male.

As time went on, a more sharply defined reform agenda emerged that linked change with the efforts of city boosters to promote Sacramento as a good place to live. Reformers insisted on honesty in government, a more stable local economy, and greater efficiency in public and private ventures. McClatchy was the voice of this movement, endlessly lampooning and haranguing city leaders and policies that gave the city a bad reputation. One of McClatchy's allies was Hiram F. Johnson, the son of longtime Sacramento lawyer and legislator Grove Johnson. Hiram Johnson, who had supported Clark against Land in mayoral politics, wedded himself to the Progressive cause. His public profile as a reformer was enhanced through his work on the prosecution team of the San Francisco Graft Trials of the early 1900s. The successful prosecution of political malefactor "Boss" Abe Ruef gave birth to the California Progressive movement. Hiram Johnson would eventually be elected governor by those same forces in 1910.

Sacramento's Progressive revolt was sparked when Southern Pacific hegemony in the city was challenged by the rival Western Pacific Railroad (WP). When WP sought a route into the city and a place to build its own yards, Southern Pacific henchmen on the city council did not openly oppose the project, but did everything they could to slow it down. Encouraged by events in San Francisco and angered at blatant railroad interference in the gubernatorial election of 1906, Sacramento reformers struck back and showed their strength in October 1907 by pushing through a right-of-way for the Western Pacific Railroad. A month later, reform forces rode to a second victory when they narrowly elected Progressive Clinton F. White as mayor. White had won by denouncing Southern Pacific as a monopoly that spoiled the prospects of Sacramento's future advance. "Why not cast out the evil influences that have so long kept the city down?" White asked in his campaign speeches. C.K. McClatchy lauded the election of White as an apocalyptic event in the history of Sacramento: "This election is a triumph for right against wrong; for law against lawlessness; for the interest of the People against the grasping clutch of corporate monopoly: for better civic government in every way."

White disappointed McClatchy's hopes by lasting only two years before he returned to his private law practice. He was replaced by the man he defeated in 1907, Marshall R. Beard. Despite McClatchy's editorial groaning that Beard represented a return to "boss rule," the mayor continued the process of city improvement begun under White. Meanwhile, McClatchy turned his interests to state politics, where the Progressive movement was led by the Lincoln-Roosevelt League, a cadre of Progressive reformers that propelled Sacramentan Hiram Johnson to the governor's seat. Under Johnson, California became a showcase of Progressive reform and Sacramento whirred with new legislative initiatives, realizing many of the hopes and dreams of reformers.

A GROWING AND CHANGING CITY

Progressive era Sacramento was not only bursting with reformist hopes, but it also began to expand spatially. In 1911, Sacramento added substantial new lands to its 1849 boundaries. The chief focus of annexationist efforts was the streetcar suburb of Oak Park on the southeastern fringe of the city. Oak Park had been laid out in the 1880s by developer Edward Alsip. A neat community of small homes, businesses, and churches, it attracted a large number of Sacramentans employed in service trades, such as telephone operators and railroad workers. Other Sacramentans had been attracted to Oak Park largely because of a popular amusement park, Joyland, which included a roller coaster, a tunnel of love, and swimming pool. In 1909, long discussed annexation plans were pushed by the Oak Park Improvement Club. Likewise lands east of 31st Street, the city's back door, also became ripe for the picking of a growing Sacramento. East Sacramento, as it was known, was a mixture of homes, a school, a dairy, and a privately owned park, as well as a race track. Although less populated than Oak Park, East Sacramento stood right in the path of the city's projected eastward expansion. The campaign for annexation began in March 1910 and succeeded in convincing both Oak Park and East Sacramento residents that joining Sacramento proper would be in their best interests. In September 1911, they approved the annexation, thereby adding 6,000 acres to the city.

The heart of Sacramento's subsequent suburban growth was north of Sacramento across the American River. The sale of the old Rancho del Paso Grant in 1910 released over 44,000 acres for county development. These lands fell into the hands of O.A. Robertson, a St. Paul capitalist working with the Sacramento Valley Colonization Company, a consortium of ten investors including former

Sacramento Mayor Daniel Webster Carmichael, who established a rural idyll bearing his own name some 12 miles east of Sacramento. Another consortium of developers planned Citrus Heights also on the Del Paso grant. Earlier in the 1880s, investors had planned Orangevale and Fair Oaks, small citrus growing communities that were intended to burnish the northern state's reputation as a sunshine capital. The North Sacramento Land Company's D.W. Johnston and his son Carl E. Johnston secured a huge 4,000-acre tract that had once been grain and grazing fields. Subdividing about 2,500 acres of this property, the Johnstons laid out a small city called North Sacramento. Cut through by 100-foot wide Del Paso Boulevard, the city thrived as Sacramento's first automobile suburb. Grammar schools, businesses, and other utilities began to give the community shape and identity. By 1929, the population was estimated at 10,000. North Sacramento cherished a strong community identity for many years, until it eventually merged with a burgeoning Sacramento in 1964. Sacramento also purchased 828 acres of the Del Paso grant along Arcade Creek to be preserved as a city park. Two 18-hole golf courses now dominate the park.

GOVERNMENTAL REFORM AGAIN

In 1910, Sacramento's newly rejuvenated city government erected a handsome new city hall on I Street. Designed by architect Rudolph Herold, the brick/terra-cotta structure with a modified onion dome presided over the city plaza and

The streetcar suburb of Oak Park, shown here c. 1910, was annexed to Sacramento in 1911.

formed a link in the chain of public buildings that included the old post office/court house and later a Carnegie-funded public library.

In June 1911, as Sacramento voters pondered the fate of Oak Park, they selected 15 freeholders to rewrite the city charter yet again. The freeholders hammered out a document that called for five non-partisan, elected commissioners who would possess equal power—thereby further undercutting bossism. In a November election that re-elected Mayor Marshall Beard, voters approved the new charter. A reform-minded Municipal Voter's League pressed hard for four reform candidates with a battle ensuing as Beard and Carraghar, old city politicians, scored well in the primaries. But the Municipal League fielded an effective counter-weight with Catholics and Democrats by endorsing Michael Burke, a prominent Catholic and labor union politician. Likewise, they took advantage of voting women by endorsing Laura Johnston, who came in fifth and became the first woman elected to municipal office in Sacramento. Beard and Carraghar continued to serve, but represented the end of the old working-class ward politics. After the commission system was up and running, Sacramento adopted a civil service system in 1913, thereby ending the practice of ward bosses handing out public jobs and of appointed officials "feeding the kitty" of political associations. Gradually, a professionalized bureaucracy emerged.

The commission system, however, lasted only a short time, unable to cope with the rapid acceleration of the city's growing needs. In 1921, Sacramento again revised its charter and created a nine-member city council. The most important innovation in the new charter was the creation of a city manager's position, which installed an urban professional to oversee city life. Sacramento's first city manager was Illinois-born Clyde L. Seavey. A former journalist and member of the Sierra Club, Seavey had been strongly endorsed by the Chamber of Commerce. Seavey's reforms trimmed the budget, consolidated governmental departments, and insisted on licensing new businesses (putting fortune-tellers, hypnotists, and mesmerists out of business). Seavey also tackled the problem of urban vice by denying the Japanese licenses to operate poolrooms, closing 30 saloons, and reviving the chain gang to scare off transients. The city council was chosen by at-large voting and the mayor, no longer the strong figure of the 1893 charter, was the councilman with the highest number of votes. The end of ward elections cost the working class its power over city government. Power passed to the educated and established and those endorsed by the Chamber of Commerce.

Progressive era emphasis on city planning reflected the increased value of city property and a desire to manage city life more efficiently. To this end, city leaders engaged the services of professional city planners. In 1908, Charles Mulford Robinson, a nationally-known urban planner, visited Sacramento and proposed a city design that included streets radiating from the state capitol. In 1916, another national leader, John Nolen, provided plans for the use of Sacramento's increasingly more valuable urban space, including a re-working of the capital's grid pattern and also an ambitious program for Del Paso Park. In 1923, the city adopted its first zoning ordinance and in 1924 created the first City Planning Commission.

Former journalist Clyde L. Seavey became Sacramento's first city manager.

Although the commission was quickly disbanded after only a few months of service, in June 1926 it was revived and became integral to rational city development.

WORLD WAR I: DEMANDS FOR LOYALTY AND A NEW MOOD

Sacramento entered World War I. By the time Woodrow Wilson delivered his dramatic request for a war declaration against the Central Powers in April 1917, most Sacramentans agreed that the time had come to teach the German Kaiser and his allies a lesson. A huge turnout at the Empress Theater fanned the flames of patriotism and urged enlistment in the armed forces. In all, about 4,000 Sacramento County youth responded to their country's call, with nearly 100 dying in the conflict. Hundreds of Sacramentans on the home front offered their services to the Red Cross and sold and bought Liberty Bonds. A local Council of Defense kept a close eye for any sign of disloyalty. In the anti-German hysteria of the era, Sacramento's Lutheran church abandoned its German language services and local Irish nationalists were barred from welcoming the widow of one of the Easter Rebellion martyrs for fear of giving offense to the American alliance with Great Britain.

During World War I, Sacramento's fears of radicalism flowered once again. The city occasionally had brushes with radical groups. Bands of unemployed workers periodically descended on the city and created jitters in the press and in city government. In 1913, for example, one of these groups, Kelley's Army, marched into Sacramento and set up shop in one of the city parks. Eventually, city officials were able to bribe them to move, but not until C.K. McClatchy sufficiently raised public fears that these "bummers" threatened the city by their demands for food and shelter. In 1917, a violent explosion damaged a portion of the back porch and kitchen of the governor's mansion. City officials blamed the blast on violent elements of the International Workers of the World (IWW), a militant labor organization that had begun to attract followers on the West Coast. A number were rounded up and jailed by the federal government, but were never convicted of this bombing. Several of the detainees died of influenza in the city jail.

When the war ended in November 1918, the city erupted with joyful demonstrations. In April 1919, Sacramentans strewed the streets with golden poppies to welcome home "the returning heroes" of the 363rd Infantry of the "Fighting 91st." Hoping to win public support for a League of Nations to prevent future conflicts, President Woodrow Wilson visited Sacramento in September 1919. Taking this internationalist message into Sacramento was an act of political courage since both McClatchy and Hiram Johnson bitterly opposed American entrance into the League. Nonetheless, nearly 10,000 Sacramentans lined the tracks on R Street shouting their approval and throwing roses at Wilson and his wife Edith. "I feel you voice approval of the great covenant signed to make peace permanent in the world," the President shouted in gratitude from the back of his rail car.

The war brought a new element to Sacramento's economy: military spending. The U.S. Army's growing interest in air power sent the War Department scurrying for factories to build the biplanes that would challenge German power.

Patriotism became increasingly visible, as evidenced by this Portuguese float built by the Nunes Brothers shipbuilders for the Fourth of July parade, 1916.

One such plant, the Liberty Works near present-day North Sacramento, made the Curtiss JN-4 (Jenny) airplane for the Army Air Corps, and in 1918 Sacramento made a strong pitch to the War Department to locate a flight school in or near the Sacramento area. Military commanders agreed, and in June, Mather Field at Mills Station became the home of an airfield and training school. City leaders welcomed the new facility, not only because it brought airplanes and military personnel (both considered an interesting novelty) but also because Mather's construction and needs pumped money into the local economy. Mather Field had a relatively brief existence because the war ended that November, and the nation demobilized rapidly. Mather Field went into dormancy in 1923, with periodic use as the site of air shows, the delivery of airmail, and even as a stop-off point for Charles "Lucky Lindy" Lindbergh, who traversed the nation after his show-stopping transatlantic flight in 1927. Mather Field, later Mather Air Force Base, reopened as a military facility just prior to World War II.

SACRAMENTO AND PROHIBITION

One of the things that War Department officers demanded of Sacramento as a "price" for locating a flight school near the city was the clean up of its West End. Drinking, gambling, and prostitution raged unabated, despite periodic clean-up attempts. A high profile commission led by Simon Lubin (son of David Lubin) scored the moral squalor of the city's "dives" in 1919 and blamed their continued existence on lax police enforcement. Not much came of the furor, but moral reforms were also high on the Progressive agenda.

Sacramento had always supported the brewing industry. Henry Grau founded the Buffalo Brewing Company in 1889 and built a huge brewery on 21st Street between Q and R—once the largest brewery west of the Mississippi. Swiss brewer Frank Ruhstaller had purchased a Sacramento brewery in 1881 and produced a popular steam beer. Ruhstaller merged his holdings with Buffalo in 1897 and eventually came to dominate the new company. The popularity of these beers and the host of taverns and saloons in the city suggested that the atmosphere of the state capital was never sympathetic to either temperance or prohibition.

Since the 1850s, organizations like the Women's Christian Temperance Union and the Sons of Temperance had pressed for saloon restrictions, but saloons were popular with the mostly male working class, who treated them as social clubs. Support for prohibition of any kind from local breweries and wineries was weak. Saloons proliferated. By 1884, there were almost 400 drinking establishments, nearly 130 of them never bothering to pay for a liquor license. (Mark Twain called Sacramento "The City of Saloons.") Groups that favored prohibition (Grangers, the American Protective Association, and social moralists in the Progressive movement) attracted supporters but were never able to rise above the opposition. Rules banning the sale and consumption of alcohol never passed muster with city officials. In 1907, an effort to ban saloons from the "Homes" section of the city failed by a wide margin in a popular vote. Anti-Saloon League activity was clearly

Mather Field's engineering officers, shown here in 1918, were among those stationed at the facility, instituted during World War I.

visible, fueled by reformers and the Ministerial Association (an alliance of local Protestant clergy), but efforts spearheaded in 1914 and in 1916 by the group were turned back. As a result, when the 18th Amendment was passed in 1919, Sacramento's embrace of the dry cause was tenuous. New Year's Eve 1919 produced its share of blowout parties—before the dread hand of Prohibition formally gripped on January 17, 1920. But despite the federal directive, Sacramentans flouted the regulation. City historians note that Sacramento had a revolving door of police chiefs during the 1920s, none of whom were able to adequately handle the problem. Bootlegging seemed to go unchallenged in both city and county. Despite periodic raids and revocation of business licenses, the less than enthusiastic or consistent enforcement of the 18th Amendment allowed the secret liquor trade to flourish. It took until 1922 for Sacramento to enforce the new law. By then speakeasies and other private drinking establishments had been established and had gained general acceptance. "Virtuecrats" in Sacramento were dismayed by the city's resistance to prohibition—their organized displeasure playing a role in the popularity of the Ku Klux Klan in the California state capital.

SACRAMENTO AND THE KU KLUX KLAN

The Klan had experienced a national revival even before the United States entered the war and had taken as its pet themes Prohibition and the disparagement of Catholics and immigrants. Klan organizers had come to Sacramento in 1921, making a dramatic appearance at the city's Westminster Presbyterian Church where they approved of the minister's preaching. From his quarters in the Traveler's Hotel, Klan organizer (Kleagle) Edgar Fuller began to tap into a wide stream of pro-Prohibition and anti-Catholic sentiment that reflected itself in the numbers willing to take out Klan membership. Sacramento Klansmen attempted to portray themselves as upstanding American patriots, devoid of prejudice (they even painted a local African-American church), but clearly were suspicious of Catholic "interests" in the city and worried about the potential for radicalism.

City Manager Clyde Seavey, with the public support of McClatchy and the *Bee*, waged war on the Klan. The paper attempted to embarrass participants in the huge induction ceremonies that took place in Oak Park and in Folsom's dredgings by sending reporters to copy down license plate numbers and then revealing the owners' names in the newspaper. A raid on Southern California Klan membership headquarters also revealed the names of several Sacramento city officials: seven policemen, three fire captains, and the city harbor master. When Seavey attempted to fire them, their appealed case was brought before the city council, which refused to support the city manager. Seavey was pilloried by some as a "red" and resigned from the manager's post. He then served in state government, and in 1934 President Franklin D. Roosevelt appointed him to the Federal Power Commission.

SACRAMENTO ASSOCIATIONALISM

The Klan's appeal to many Sacramentans (hundreds showed up for the induction ceremonies) certainly was related to the fears and reaction of the postwar period. Progressivism had spent its energies, and people were anxious for the comfort of the "old times" promised by Klan rhetoric. But the Klan's popularity was also related to the organization's fraternal appeal. Sacramentans were joiners and had a strong network of fraternal organizations that bonded businessmen and fellow citizens in collective endeavors.

Close associations often began in the city high school where students formed sororities and fraternities. Fraternal groups like the Howards and the Odd Fellows made a significant contribution to the emergence of city benevolence to the poor and to professional health care. Strong Masonic lodges developed and banded together for charitable as well as political reasons. Likewise groups like the Elks, the Improved Order of Redmen, and the Knights of Pythias built substantial meeting halls. Irish citizens could join the Ancient Order of Hibernians, and young Catholic men and women could participate in the Young Men's and Young Women's Institutes. Singers could warble with the McNeill Club. Ethnic communities like the Germans formed the *Turnverein*, while the Portuguese formed devotional societies like the *Irmandade do Divino Espirito Santo (IDES)*, which underwrote annual festivals and celebrations.

One Sacramento association that has stood the test of time is the Sutter Club, founded in 1889 with rules drawn up by Valentine McClatchy and Judge William Cary Van Fleet. The founders were up and coming (and in some cases quite accomplished) professionals in business, law, medicine, and agriculture. Desiring a better place to meet, socialize, and discuss affairs than the rough and tumble haunts on Front Street, the new club began its operation in the upper room of the California State Bank on Fourth and J Streets. Later, the association built a clubhouse on Ninth and L, once the site of a Baptist church. Their annual Christmas ball was one of the social highlights of Sacramento's year. Nearly all the city's civic leaders were members and the roster read like a *Who's Who* of Sacramento elite.

Another popular gathering spot was the country club, which meant the Del Paso Country Club. Originally called the Sacramento Golf Club, in 1916 it moved from its headquarters to a location on the old Rancho del Paso. Here city residents met for golf, tennis, trapshooting, and dances. For Sacramento women, the major social gathering was the Tuesday Club, founded December 1, 1896. A second group dedicated to cultural advancement among Sacramento women was the Saturday Club.

TOWARD A GREATER SACRAMENTO

The fears of Sacramentans, reflected in their embrace of harsh measures against radicals and membership in the Klan, was counterbalanced by their wholesale embrace of modernity. Leading the charge to modernize Sacramento life were the collective forces of the Chamber of Commerce. Under executive secretary Harry Muddox, the chamber made great strides in improving the city and in attracting federal dollars. In 1922, Muddox stepped down and was replaced by one of the most indefatigable of Sacramento's boosters, Arthur Serviss Dudley.

Dudley was a native of West Salem, Wisconsin and a graduate of the Illinois College of Photography. Attracted by a career in boosterism, he became secretary of the Riverside Chamber of Commerce and later took a similar position in Los Angeles. He arrived in Sacramento in 1920 as secretary to the chamber and helped pull the city's development energies together. To unite the city, Dudley drew memories of the past into the service of a new modernized Sacramento, which he believed needed civic unity. He hosted a huge historical festival called the "Days of '49" adjacent to the rail yards on the site of the present-day railroad depot in May 1922. It featured a "whiskerino" contest for which some Sacramento men had grown beards for six months. For the occasion, event planners constructed a mining town, an Indian village, and a wooden mountain that offered donkey rides. Fireworks, parades, rodeos, and music also punctuated the event. "Sacramento has reincarnated the spirit of the Days of '49," crowed an account of the celebration. "The march of life, the very atmosphere of the romantic days of the Argonauts has been brought back." The message was nostalgic but the goals thoroughly modern: Sacramento had to pull itself together for the task of urban improvement and civic growth. Dudley later played a pivotal role in the economic development of Sacramento, recruiting and helping initiate the development of infrastructure, buildings, and greater employment opportunities.

TRANSPORTATION AND THE RISE OF AUTOMOBILE CULTURE

As people-moving technology improved, Sacramento became increasingly connected with a wider area. A series of inter-urban lines ran back and forth from the state capital, connecting the city with Chico, San Francisco, Woodland, and other cities. Sacramento gradually eased into one of its most significant social changes with its embrace of the automobile. In 1900, the first automobile was exhibited at one of the city's periodic street fairs. In 1902, car races were held for the first time in the city, and in 1903, merchant Joseph Schnerr leased a shop on Tenth and J for the sale of automobiles and bicycles. By the next year, 27 automobiles were registered in Sacramento. By 1910, the number had leapt to 700, and in 1912 there were 16 automobile agencies, 1 assembly plant, and 11 garages. By 1929, one in three Sacramentans owned a car. Trucks and buses made their appearance in 1910. A bus route between Sacramento and Folsom opened in 1910; in 1914, buses connected the city with Stockton. Trucking firms also began to move in on the short-haul traffic generally carried by the railroads. The advent of the automobile ended the work of horseshoers, blacksmiths, wagon makers, and feed and harness stores. Ultimately, the vehicles undermined the powerful railroad and ended the steamboat era.

The creation of a network of passable and interconnected roads became a state priority in 1895 when a committee was established to draw up a plan. In 1895 as

The Days of '49 celebration in 1922 featured a constructed mining town, an Indian village, and a wooden mountain that offered donkey rides.

well, the state purchased the Lake Tahoe Wagon Toll Road, which became the skeleton of Highway 50, connecting Sacramento with the popular resort area. The state created the California Highway Commission in 1909, which secured a bond issue financing the construction of the Yolo Causeway, an elevated two-lane roadway propped up by a wooden infrastructure. This dependable land link with the Bay Area opened in 1916.

A group of local bicycle aficionados formed the Capital City Wheelmen in 1886, and during their races became aware of the perilous conditions around the state capital. After taking inventory, the Wheelmen made common cause with local merchants and held a Good Roads Convention in 1903. But funding new roads posed problems. An early effort to vote bond money for a road project ran into Supreme Court opposition; however, in 1907 a successful bond issue was passed that began a network of paved roads, including the major laterals out of the city: Folsom Boulevard, Stockton and Franklin Boulevards, Auburn Boulevard, part of Riverside Boulevard, and Jackson Road to Plymouth. In 1911–1912, new bridges spanned the American River: the 12th Street Bridge and the H Street Bridge. In 1916, additional bond money was made available for further improvements and bridge construction.

THE BUILDING BOOM OF THE 1920s

Civic pride and World War I patriotism combined to re-work the built-space of Sacramento in the early decades of the twentieth century. According to historians Paula Boghosian and Bonnie Snyder, nearly 30 new buildings were erected to beautify the downtown. In 1918, a new Carnegie library was built on I Street next to the City Plaza. On or near J Street alone the following new buildings went up: the D.O. Mills Bank, the Capital National Bank, the Masonic Temple at 12th and J with its glowering sculpted Knights Templar, the Public Market at 13th and J, the California Western Life Insurance building at Ninth and J, and the Elks Building on 11th and J. The crowning achievement of the decade was the Memorial Auditorium completed in 1927 on 16th and J. Designed by architects Dean & Dean, the Memorial Auditorium honored the heroes of World War I and was the city's public center and the site of entertainments as diverse as operatic performances, boxing matches, and big band orchestras. Added to these new structures were the Southern Pacific Depot at Third and I and the graceful granite Capitol Extension buildings that faced each other west of the state house.

A raft of church buildings also began to grace the state capital. Many of them had originally been on the city's deteriorating West End but relocated east of the riverfront. Sacramento's first church, the First Congregational, had been torn down in the early 1920s and a new building, resembling the old, was built near Sutter's Fort. The members of the First Methodist Episcopal built an elegant church on the corner of 21st and J, but most dramatic was the Westminster Presbyterian Church with its Byzantine-like dome, which rose south of Capitol Park. Likewise, the beautiful First Baptist Church on 24th and L soon dominated its city space. In 1922, Sacramento's Catholic bishop, Patrick Keane, urged the Christian Brothers to sell their decaying property on the corner of 12th and K where it had been since 1876. The brothers eventually relocated their popular school to 21st and Broadway, and on the old Christian Brothers site, the Weinstock, Lubin & Company store relocated from its historical Fourth and J location into an elegant new store modeled after the Parisian department store *Le Printemps*.

Health care professionals also sought to reinvigorate the city's antiquated health care system. Even before World War I and the deadly Spanish Influenza epidemic that hit the city with gale force in 1918, city physicians had been pressing for a new hospital. An elaborate plan was worked out with the Sisters of Mercy and the local physician's association to build such a structure (to be named Memorial Hospital in honor of the city's World War I veterans), but these negotiations fell apart. In the aftermath of the collapsed deal, a consortium of physicians erected Sutter Hospital in 1923. Undaunted by the increased financial risks, the Sisters of Mercy followed through on their plans and transferred their health care facility to former dairy lands on 40th and J Streets. Designed by city hall architect Rudolph Herold, Sisters Hospital (Mater Misericordiae) opened in 1925. In the 1930s, it changed its name to Mercy Hospital.

Electric street railways made suburban development possible. Handsome residential areas developed in East Sacramento as developers Charles Wright and Howard Kimbrough, in business since 1892, moved into the "back door" of the growing city. By this time the city's fascination with Victorian homes was done. A

The Elks Temple was one of the city's first skyscrapers.

91

Sutter Hospital was erected by a consortium of physicians after World War I.

brief infatuation with craftsmen style homes and various "revival" styles of housing architecture reflected itself in the new urban housing stock. Wright and Kimbrough developed Tract 24, an expansive housing subdivision later known as the Fabulous Forties. Historian Kerry Philips has observed the new technology of home building during this time with better plumbing, utilities, and spatial efficiency—as well as more developed notions of health, family size, and privacy inherent in the new homes. Tract 24 sported Southern style mansions, villas, and mission-style homes set in from the tree-lined streets that became the residence of choice for Sacramento's upwardly mobile elites. Meanwhile, Christopher Jones, Wilbur Brand, and Frank Williams formed the Sierra Oaks Development Corporation and along H Street transformed the formerly bucolic area into a tract of beautiful homes.

Likewise, evolution of the city's water plans led to the removal of the old Y Street Levee. Y Street was renamed Broadway in 1938 and south of it William Land Park, a plot of land purchased with a handsome bequest from a former mayor and hotelier, took shape. Around the beautiful park, a series of small homes and comfortable residences took shape. Likewise the area around Sacramento City College on Freeport Boulevard blossomed with new developments. Next door to Land Park was Curtis Park, a neighborhood that grew in the shadow of the Western Pacific yards.

Schools too were making their appearance in greater number. A successful bond issue in 1921 resulted in a new Sacramento High School completed three years later. This state of the art school was the single most important educational entity in the city. Additional spending approved in 1921 resulted in six new elementary schools. The capstone, though, was the establishment of a junior college. The new college originally met in the upper floor of the old Sacramento High School until a bond issue in the 1920s made possible the construction of new buildings on Freeport Boulevard. Public subscriptions erected Hughes Stadium, home of the City College Panthers, and contributed to Sacramento's growing love for spectator sports. Events at Hughes Field helped unite the burgeoning city. In later years, the annual football match between the rival city high schools—Sacramento High and McClatchy High—would be waged on Thanksgiving Day.

In 1924, the McGeorge School of Law opened in Sacramento, providing legal training for local citizens. In 1966, the school affiliated itself with the Stockton-based University of the Pacific. Dean Gordon Schaber joined the faculty in 1953 and eventually became a Sacramento Superior Court judge and dean of the growing school. Well known in Sacramento for his civic activism, he became a respected figure in the community. McGeorge faculty member Anthony M. Kennedy, son of a respected legal family, reached the heights of the American judiciary when President Gerald Ford named him to the Ninth Circuit in 1975. In 1988, President Ronald Reagan appointed him to the Supreme Court.

NEW INFRASTRUCTURE

"Sacramento's impure water supply [is] one of the greatest obstacles to growth of the city," noted a Chamber of Commerce report in 1895. City water was still undrinkable; as one resident recalled, "The water came out of the faucet almost a brick red." Individual Sacramentans attempted to purify it with home devices such as Pasteur filters and holding tanks that allowed the sediment to sink to the bottom. The city improved the water considerably when they agreed to chlorinate it. Yet it was not until 1915 that a report presented to the Board of Trustees urged that Sacramento use river water and that proper filtration be implemented to make the water "brilliantly clear, colorless, satisfactorily soft, and hygienically most gratifying and safe." In June 1919, voters approved a bond issue of $1.8 million for the new filtration plant. Situated near the Jibboom Street Bridge, the handsome plant had etched on its cornice the words of the Prophet Ezechiel, "And everything shall live whithersoever the river cometh." On December 31, 1923, President Calvin Coolidge pressed a button in Washington, D.C., that electrified Sacramento's city plaza and caused clear water to gush forth from the fountain, heralding the completion of the city's new filtration plant. Sacramento had always had legal rights to the abundant waters of the Sacramento and American Rivers and their tributaries in mountain streams. Now, as mermaids frolicked in the city plaza fountain, Sacramento finally had a supply of clean water.

Aligned with the need for more water was the need for more electricity. In 1921, the state legislature approved the creation of municipal utility districts with the power to raise money. Voters in 1923 approved the formation of a publicly owned utility company, the Sacramento Municipal Utility District (SMUD) to implement the city's claim to water and power rights on Silver Creek in El Dorado County. However, privately-owned PG&E and Great Western utility companies refused to give up their hold on water and hydroelectric generation in Sacramento. SMUD tried in vain to purchase facilities for generation, and three separate bond issues fell short of the necessary two-thirds majority needed for the construction of a dam. However, the building of the Central Valley Project in the 1930s contributed to sentiment in favor of publicly owned power. SMUD also continued to add various localities to its service area, expanding its ability to pass bond issues. After years of litigation and negotiation, SMUD took over the operation of Sacramento's electric distribution system from PG&E on December 31, 1946. The utility providers arrived just as a new wave of growth would place tremendous demands on Sacramento's power supply.

CITY JOURNALISM, ENTERTAINMENT, AND LEISURE

During this time, the *Sacramento Bee* became the dominant daily, outdistancing its longtime rival, the *Union*. The paper accomplished its goals by responding to a variety of different constituencies in the Sacramento Valley, including calling it "Superior California." Under the solid financial leadership of Valentine McClatchy, the *Bee* substantially increased its readership by an innovative "block-subscription" marketing strategy and attracted more advertising accounts. The popular evening daily managed to walk a fine line between its crusading editorializing and the sensibilities of local panjandrums who might be offended by C.K.'s sometimes trenchant rhetoric. The paper took over the rival Scripps-owned *Sacramento Star* in 1924, and for the first time the *Bee* had popular funny pages.

The rival *Sacramento Union* maintained its niche as the morning daily of the city and the chief rival to the *Bee*'s dominance. As the city's communication giant, the *Bee* was the natural source for the introduction of radio to the city. Two stations shared the same radio frequency; KVQ and the *Bee*-operated KFBK began broadcasting from the Kimball-Upson Building on K Street on September 23, 1922.

Only a handful of theaters existed in Sacramento as the new century dawned: the Clunie, the Acme Theater, the Grand, and the Alisky Theater. By the early 1900s, Sacramento theaters provided a mix of popular vaudeville and stock dramatic productions. By 1913, ten theaters were to be found on K Street. However, even though vaudeville would continue to play in Sacramento until the 1930s, these venues began to lose their appeal as talking movies became popular. When the majestic Clunie was torn down in 1923, Guy B. Post, an actor who had played on its stage in the early twentieth century, viewed the ruins and remarked, "What a desecration." Ironically, as historian Andrew Flink notes, he was in town to promote his movie, "Gold Madness."

Movies supplanted stage and vaudeville productions as one of Sacramento's most popular pastimes. Sacramento's first movie was George Melies "Trip to the Moon," which debuted March 9, 1903 in Grauman's Vaudeville Theater. A local entrepreneur, Charles W. Godard, came to control a number of city theaters and took a major hand in retooling them to show motion pictures. In 1915, he opened his own theater (modestly named the Godard), which became the first

Sacramento theater devoted to the full-time screening of motion pictures. Fox West Coast Theaters began to dominate the city's movie theater market, taking over the Hippodrome on K Street (today the Crest) in 1928 along with several other downtown theaters. Ethnic theaters included the Mexico, which operated from 1930 to 1933, and the Nippon, a Japanese movie house.

Movie theaters had their historic moments. The controversial film, *Birth of a Nation* (billed as *The Clansman*), appeared at the Clunie. In March 1928, the Capitol Theater gave Sacramento its first talking picture, *The Jazz Singer* with Al Jolson. Sacramento theaters also became more comfortable and patron-friendly. One of the most elegant was the Alhambra, designed by architects Leonard Stark and Edward Flanders to resemble a Moorish castle. The exotic architecture, the gardens, the courtyards, and the small oranges hanging from the trees, as well as quotations from *The Rubaiyat of Omar Khayyam*, made movie-going a total sensory experience. In 1938, the "thoroughly modern" Tower Theater was built on the fringe of the Land Park district.

Sacramento also became a popular site for Hollywood filmmaking. Between 1914 and 1935, Sacramento area locales provided the backdrop for 45 feature length films such as *Huckleberry Finn*, *Show Boat*, and *Steamboat 'Round the Bend*. Famous directors who visited Sacramento include King Vidor, Cecile B. DeMille, and John Ford. While Hollywood directors favored the Sacramento River for its cinematographic verisimilitude, in fact the use of the river for pleasure craft was not just a celluloid dream. Well into the 1930s, two paddle wheel steamers, the *Delta Queen* and *Delta King*, plied the waters of the Sacramento offering food,

The elegant Alhambra Theatre resembled a Moorish castle.

lodging, entertainment, and gambling. Although eventually taken out of service for lack of passengers, for many years the vessels provided a tangible reminder of Sacramento's early transportation history.

Public entertainment also included taking advantage of the little slices of nature within the built environment of Sacramento—city parks. In 1911, a $250,000 legacy from former mayor and hotelier William Land mandated the selection of a park site. The city purchased 236 acres of the Swanston-McDevitt Tract between Riverside and Freeport Boulevards in 1918. Land's heirs balked at the purchase of "remote" swampland and a strong campaign sought to reverse the acquisition and transfer the Land bequest to rural Del Paso Park. (There was even a citywide vote in its favor). However, a court battle resolved only in 1922 insisted that the purchase was permanent, and the park began to take shape. The city built a new levee, drained wetlands, planted 4,000 trees and 6,000 shrubs, laid out a nine hole golf course, and opened William Land Park. Sculptures and fountains were donated for its beautification. As a suburban neighborhood developed around the beautiful park, it quickly became one of Sacramento's finest and soon added a city zoo and a children's recreation park called Fairy Tale Town.

By the late 1920s, Sacramento's population edged closer to the 100,000 mark hoped for by developers. In 1928, the annual meeting of the state Association of Realtors was held in Sacramento, and visiting agents noted, "Sacramento [had] struck her real stride in the development of a modern metropolis and the building of a real skyline." In a myriad of statistics, from water connections to school enrollments, the future seemed bright and beautiful for California's state capital.

The movie Steamboat 'Round the Bend *with Will Rogers was filmed in Sacramento in 1935. Insert shows Rogers chatting with Buck McKee of Roseville.*

5. THE NEW DEAL AND THE WAR

Nearly 15,000 Sacramentans crowded the Southern Pacific Depot in September 1932 to catch a glimpse of Franklin Delano Roosevelt, the Democratic nominee for President. As New York governor, Roosevelt motored down K Street on a whirlwind tour of the business district, the state capitol, and Sutter's Fort, thousands thronged his route. A local band played his campaign theme song, "Happy Days are Here Again," but social and economic conditions in California's capital were anything but happy.

THE GRIP OF THE DEPRESSION

If the crowds had permitted him, FDR, soon to be elected to the presidency, may have seen some of the shacks of the unemployed near the rail yards. The economic and social devastation of the Great Depression was painfully evident in Sacramento. Unemployment first hit the seasonal canning industry. Already in September 1930, 153 employees of the California Cooperative Producers Canning Company had been turned out of their jobs without pay as demand plummeted for canned goods. Ultimately, the once prosperous company found itself $25,000 in arrears to 600 seasonal employees. Angry workers filed petitions at the State Labor Bureau but to no avail. Added to the misery caused by market downturns, nature itself waged war on the local fruit and canning industries when a terrible freeze hit valley citrus crops in early December 1932, destroying at least half of the citrus trees—especially oranges. Cannery officials struggled to keep operations going and promised city officials that they would give work only to residents. In 1933, local residents were heartened when the canneries began an aggressive hiring program. However, such optimism was short-lived when cannery officials decided to take advantage of the glutted and desperate job market by paying workers as little as 20¢ per hour; less than $10 a week for six eight-hour days.

Cannery workers were not alone. By December 22, 1931, local banks were promising financial assistance to school teachers and all county employees whose salary warrants had been postponed until January. Employment problems multiplied. Workers at the two rail yards experienced layoffs and reduced workweeks. In 1931, the Western Pacific shops laid off two-thirds of its workers.

As the Democratic nominee for President, Franklin Delano Roosevelt visited Sacramento in September 1932.

Later in the year, the shops reopened with a skeleton crew of 200, working a four-day week. In early February 1932, the desperation of the increasing number of unemployed burst on the public scene when local newspapers recorded a mini-riot of 200 men all scrambling for 20 temporary jobs unloading heavy granite from a flatcar to river barges. "The twenty best fighters completed the work and drew their pay early in the afternoon," observed the local press. Unemployment skyrocketed. Adding to the distress, two Sacramento banks—the California National Bank and the California Trust and Savings Bank—failed to open on January 21, 1933. Heavy withdrawals had begun, culminating in a bank run on the Friday before the closing, drawing the banks's reserves below their legal limit. By 1932, there were 27,000 unemployed in Sacramento.

Adding to the mix of unemployed residents of Sacramento was the presence of a large number of transients who set up "Hoovervilles" or transient camps. In order to discourage them from going to the city's shelter, which had begun feeding the homeless, City Manager Dean banned all feeding, even when donors appeared with tubs of beans and loaves of bread. Transients, nonetheless, only increased in numbers as the desperation spread across the nation. In 1935, a state survey taken of California's transients noted that nearly 3,000 lived in shanty villages "almost within the shadow of the capitol dome." Researchers identified several different areas, mostly along the route of the railroad tracks. In the area around the Jibboom

Street Bridge many homeless camped and built shelters. Near the city incinerator with its piles of rotting garbage was a district called Shooksville, where nearly 1,000 people of all races, age groups, and nationalities lived. Named for Samuel Shooks, an African American who was hailed as "mayor" of the area, Shooksville contended constantly with rodents, flies, and mosquitoes drawn by the rotting garbage (from which transients also picked meals and salvaged junk) as well as stagnant pools of water. Along Y Street, several groups of seasonal workers—Finns, Mexicans, and Russians—lived a quasi-communal life when times were slow in the fields or the mines. On 20th Street was an area known as the "Rattlesnake District." Huddled here were mostly young, single men, many of them ex-convicts who lived in dampness and mud from the overflow of the spring rains. On 25th Street, Sacramento's traditional "hobo jungle" was another small colony.

As the number of unemployed grew, city and county government could or would do little. For many years, city council leaders had taken a laissez faire approach to many city problems. As noted earlier, when they came under pressure from local newspapers, churches, and women's groups to clean up vice, they did little. The office of mayor, filled by the council person with the most votes in an election year, was largely a ceremonial task. Real power resided with the city manager who at the time of the Great Depression was James S. Dean, a local architect who remained at the post until 1943. But even he was unable to confront this crisis head-on. The city had no agency responsible for relief, but instead relied on the network of private charitable organizations that had traditionally been the city's social safety net: the Salvation Army, the Ann Land Memorial Fund, the Isador Cohen Fund (which provided shoes for needy children), the Catholic Ladies Relief Society, and other sectarian organizations. Twenty-two of these organizations received substantial donations from the highly popular Community Chest, which raised thousands during the prosperous 1920s.

Faith in private sector solutions was also propagated by local business leaders who sought to be cheerleaders for the ailing local economy and formed a committee on unemployment. Private unemployment exchanges, "outsourcing" the care of the indigent to the agencies of the Community Chest, and above all helping to curb the "psychology" of depression were some of the ideas put forward by the committee in November 1930. City leaders picked up on this. City Manager Dean expressed their spirit when he urged a better psychological outlook, because after all, "it [the Depression] would not last." City council members suggested hiring the unemployed for neglected home repairs and even recommended that unemployed Sacramentans consider the example of New Yorkers who sold apples on the street.

But the inadequacy of private initiatives was painfully evident as the Depression only got worse. Serious problems at the city's homeless shelter at Front and I Streets accentuated the problems with privatizing charity. Located in the old city waterworks, the shelter was operated by the city recreation department with funds from the Community Chest. However, once the demands on the shelter grew, officials turned its direction over to the Salvation Army. Angry homeless men protested the decision, rejecting the Salvation Army's liberal doses of religion served with the soup they dished out.

Faith in private sector initiatives to combat poverty were shaken even more in November 1930, when the Community Chest announced it would be $32,000 short of its goal. Community Chest collections plummeted even further in 1932, when the appeal fell short by $100,000. Chest officers cut the budget 35 percent and jettisoned their "quality of life" donations. By early January 1932, the number of family relief cases handled by Community Chest agencies had increased from 496 in December 1931 to 1,011. In May, the Chest simply ran out of money and turned all their cases over to the county.

COUNTY RESPONSES

City officials must have been puzzled by the stubborness of the Depression, but they could take some solace in the fact that under California law, relief of the poor was not a city but a county responsibility. Here too, however, the structure of relief efforts was inadequate for the demands of the time. Public relief was administered by a small county office that dispensed a limited number of goods and also relied on the county poor farm and poor house to pick up the slack. Sacramento's registrar of charities for years was the doughty Mary Judge, a single woman who administered the tiny welfare office. Under her wing were not only care for the indigent but also relief for senior citizens and aid for widows and the blind. Judge was a gruff and forbidding woman who nonetheless had a heart of gold. She often helped indigents out of her own pocket after unceremoniously ejecting them from the county office.

Judge's handle on local welfare needs was marked by the old-fashioned informality that reigned in Sacramento for many years. A longtime resident of Sacramento, she knew most of the indigents in the county and believed that she could separate the worthy from the unworthy. Transients of any kind, a serious problem because of the sheer numbers who came into the city "riding the rails," were given the back of her hand and perhaps a boot out of the locality. Judge lamented the advent of the automobile, which only increased the problem of transiency. By rail, car, or foot, the transients kept coming, and there was no money to help them. Not only had the Community Chest dried up, but tax revenue had withered as well. County assessments also showed a decline, as did city revenues. Tax delinquencies skyrocketed. Judge seized the moment with characteristic toughness and declared that only Sacramento residents would be given relief—all others would have to depart. To save money, she abandoned monetary relief and began to dispense rations, expending $5 per week for a family of five.

But Judge's "get tough" tactics reached their limits. Angry groups of unemployed banded together to form an Unemployed Council to pressure city and county officials for more food, lodging, and bathing facilities. Dissatisfaction with the amount of city and county relief led to angry gatherings, and in early 1933, a group of 100 men descended on Judge's offices. Judge faced the mob down and then heard them as they begged for additional help, the dispensing of the "work test" as a way of getting food, and freedom from police harassment that prevented them from even discussing politics. In July 1933, a near riot erupted when a number of the hungry and homeless, many of them transients, again stormed Judge's office. This time she called for law enforcement.

The militancy of the unemployed created a backlash among the city's leaders, especially in the police department, led by Chief William A. Hallanan. A hunger march held in April 1934 brought accusations of communist influence. In the late summer of that year, a raid on communist headquarters in Sacramento led to the arrest of 24 persons. Seventeen were charged and fourteen actually went to trial, accused of vagrancy and criminal syndicalism. Sacramento District Attorney J.W. Babcock built strong public opinion against the defendants before they even set foot in the courtroom. These trials became a showcase for political statements from both sides as widely irrelevant issues were injected. The Sacramento trials resulted in the conviction of eight of the fourteen. Nevertheless, Sacramento's economic problems did not go away by simply tagging protestors "communist" or "socialist." Even before the trials, Sacramento leaders had begun to realize that relief could not be dispensed as it had been in the past. Grudgingly, in 1933, Judge allowed Sacramento Board of Supervisors clerk Earl Desmond to move into her office and begin a new filing system. New measures and new income were needed.

Although Sacramento had been the temporary beneficiary of federal largesse in Mather Field and road construction, for the first time, the city had to turn to Washington, D.C. for help in dealing with what had always been a local responsibility: social welfare. The city applied for $23,000 in government assistance with the Reconstruction Finance Corporation (RFC), a Hoover-era program devised to help reignite business. The RFC loan along with other government programs began to direct money back into Sacramento. With the election of Franklin Delano Roosevelt in 1932 and the commencement of the myriad of New Deal programs, the direct impact of the federal government on the city and people of Sacramento increased substantially.

GOVERNMENT PROGRAMS TO THE RESCUE

Several New Deal programs poured money into Sacramento. Some federal funds, especially for transients, came through the State Employment Relief Administration (SERA). SERA's help with the transients enabled the cash-strapped city to feed and clothe them. SERA also helped to coordinate the flow of federal dollars that came from other New Deal agencies. The Civil Works Administration, begun in the first months of the Roosevelt Administration, provided Sacramento with a few needed infrastructure projects. County executive Charles W. Deterding proposed a loan of $130,000 to add bridges on Lower Stockton Road (Franklin Boulevard) and a clinic building at the County Hospital. Federal aid also came to the state for a variety of local projects in late 1934, including road grading for city streets, improvement of hospital grounds, tree removal, golf course cleanup, and the installation of street signs and traffic signals. Likewise, the construction of the landmark Tower Bridge in 1935 was made possible by a transfer from the Civil Works Administration. In January 1934, the Public Works Administration (PWA) approved a loan of $340,000 to build a new Home for Aged Women on the grounds of the County Hospital. C.K. McClatchy High School on Freeport Boulevard and the auditorium of the City College were also built with PWA funds. In all the PWA pumped in $3 million to Sacramento.

But the biggest donor to the city's infrastructure was the Works Progress Administration (WPA), created by the Roosevelt Administration in 1935 and overseen by social worker Harry Hopkins. WPA projects benefited the entire county and included 46 new public buildings, over 220 miles of new highway and streets, improvements in William Land and Del Paso Parks, 14 new exhibition halls and administration buildings at the state fairgrounds, and additional runways at McClellan Field and the Municipal Airport. The beautification and upgrading of Sacramento gave the aging city a new look. Symbolic of the changes was the renaming of M Street into the grandiloquent Capitol Avenue in 1940. WPA workers provided hours of cataloguing and indexing of state records, books and newspapers, and vital statistics—including old city records dating from 1849. Historical materials for various California counties were inventoried along with materials in the state Indian exhibit.

The construction of the landmark Tower Bridge, shown here when it opened in 1935, was made possible by the Civil Works Administration.

Federal money enhanced the cultural infrastructure of Sacramento as well. Under the auspices of the Federal Art Project, directed by Joseph Briton Matthew of the City College's art department, some of the famed New Deal art was created for public places. The newly built auditorium of the City College was adorned with a mural painted by Bay Area artist Ralph Stackpole. Stackpole, heavily influenced by Mexican muralist Diego Rivera, had also sculpted fountains for William Land Park and the city plaza. Artist Kathryn Uhl Ball's drawings and watercolors of Sacramento buildings were also a legacy of this era. A short-lived Sacramento Art Center offered classes and exhibits at various locations. In addition a Sacramento Federal Orchestra offered free concerts to area residents while orchestral training was provided at the Oak Park Library. By the time the WPA office closed in June 1942, over $4 million had been pumped into Sacramento County.

Equally important, the approval of the massive Central Valley Project in 1937, and its extension to the American River watershed in 1944, began a long-awaited systematization of the river, water, and energy systems of the Sacramento Valley. This included the building of levees and plans for a dam at Folsom, making possible a safe system of flood control. The surge of federal funding was only the beginning of a long-term relationship with the federal government, as the Roosevelt era transformed the relationship between the federal government and American cities. An ongoing array of federally mandated and funded programs soon became an important part of urban life in the California capital. The energetic Chamber of Commerce, under the leadership of Arthur S. Dudley, usually simply pro-business, aggressively lobbied for federal funds.

DUDLEY: PROMOTER OF AIR POWER

Although Dudley had left Sacramento for short stints as an urban booster in Stockton and in Oregon, he returned to the city permanently in 1927 and resumed his work with the Chamber of Commerce. It was Dudley's lobbying that brought the single most important change to Sacramento's economy: military installations. City developers like Dudley and others looked enviously on the impact of military installations on locales like San Diego, San Francisco, and Los Angeles. Sacramento had had its brief flirtation with a military base when Mather Field opened in 1918. However, the base was almost immediately downsized once World War I was over. Although it lingered through the 1920s as a base for airmail and was resuscitated in the early 1930s when the government staged war games over Sacramento, the federal government permanently closed it down in 1932 as a budget saving measure.

Dudley knew how to lobby. He had helped keep March Field alive in Los Angeles and determined to do the same for Mather. Even before Mather closed, Dudley had begun shuttling regularly to Washington to lobby for commercial air routes. On one of his trips he met *Sacramento Bee* correspondent Gladstone Williams. Williams put him in touch with General Henry "Hap" Arnold, who was waging a strong campaign to enhance the role of the air force. Through Arnold he met maverick military men like Generals Billy Mitchell and Carl Spatz, who also urged the resistant military establishment to build a credible American air force. Joining private business support to their military perspective, Dudley argued that a larger air force would require logistical centers located at strategic places scattered throughout the country—especially along the coastal areas—locations that were more vulnerable to attack.

In November 1934, Dudley joined forces with fellow Chamber of Commerce secretary Reginald Waters of Miami to create the National Air Defense Frontier Association, a lobbying firm that mobilized chambers of commerce around the nation to press for a series of supply and logistical centers for the Army Air Corps on the coasts of the United States. Bombarding legislators, public officials, and military men with studies and requests for more military air preparedness, Dudley and his associates achieved success in the early 1930s with the approval of a plan to create a ring of 20 air bases as a foundation for continental defense. Making league with Florida Democratic Congressman J. Mark Wilcox, they aided in drafting a bill to create new air bases at strategic coastal locations. Senator Hiram Johnson of California pushed the bill through the Senate, and it became law in 1935. Appropriating the money took time, but the matter was pressed effectively by local Congressman Frank Buck. Before the money came through, Dudley urged Alden Anderson, president of the Capital National Bank and a Chamber of Commerce official, to snap up lands that might be available for an air depot. Anderson dispatched an agent from the firm of Artz and Cook to obtain options on 1,200 acres on the old Rancho del Paso at the low price of $111,855. When the money came through and the selection panel chose Sacramento as the site for one of the new air depots, the community was ready to move.

On September 8, 1936, at ceremonies presided over by Governor Frank Merriam, the army began construction of the base, soon to be named for Hezekiah McClellan, an Indiana army pilot who died in a test crash in 1936. To the new site were transferred men, supplies, and materiel from the Rockwell Air Depot in San Diego. The new arrivals flowed in between December 1938 and January 1939. In April 1939, the base was dedicated. Conceived as a supply and aircraft maintenance base, it was one of the best equipped in the nation. Completed just as World War II was beginning, the base soon grew rapidly. The workweek was expanded to round-the-clock operations, and the base became one of Sacramento's major employers of women. By 1943, women had been promoted to the all-male preserve of production inspectors. Its employment force zoomed to over 22,000 by 1943 but declined predictably after the end of World War II.

An unexpected bonus was the re-opening of Mather Field, which a generous congress re-established in May 1936. Mather was chosen as a training facility for navigators and new buildings were constructed north of its original site. In 1941, a class of 46 navigators (including two Sacramentans) reported for school at the base. In 1958, it was selected as a base for the Strategic Air Command. Employment numbers hovered between 6,000 and 7,000, with more military than civilian wage earners.

Sacramento booster Arthur S. Dudley greets "Hap Arnold," 1930.

In 1942 the army spun off a Sacramento-based sub-depot of the Quartermaster Corps to reduce congestion at the San Francisco–Oakland Port of Embarkation. Later the Signal Corps took charge of the depot, and the site became an important storage and repair location for army communications equipment. Eventually the depot moved from its initial location at the State Fairgrounds on Broadway and Stockton Boulevard to temporary quarters at the Bercut-Richards packing plant in the northwest part of the city. In 1945, the army constructed permanent facilities for the depot on a 485-acre site 8 miles southeast of the capital. Its workforce peaked at 4,000 mostly civilian employees in 1968. McClellan, Mather, and the Signal Depot soon became major economic players in Sacramento County, and their locations outside of the city limits stimulated even more suburban development.

THE WAR

Sacramentans learned of the air raid on Pearl Harbor late in the morning of Sunday, December 7, 1941. By 2 p.m. hundreds of workers were ordered to McClellan Field to begin outfitting B-26s and P-40s for shipment to Alaska. City government coordinated emergency plans. Mayor Thomas Monk organized civil defense procedures and beefed up security around public buildings, keeping a vigilant eye on Delta levees for signs of sabotage. The first blackout mandated by civil defense authorities took place one day after Pearl Harbor Day at 7:23 in the evening. Nevertheless, not everyone heard the order; city display windows and even the water tower lights remained lit. Subsequent efforts resulted in similar patterns of erratic non-compliance—including the continued lighting of Sacramento's 14-story Elks Building. Eventually, a county ordinance was passed establishing an adequate system of signaling blackouts and informing people when they were over. By 1943, over 14,000 Sacramentans had signed on as Civil Defense volunteers.

Sacramentans once again became used to uniformed men walking their downtown streets. Local residents were urged to welcome the lads. The popular United Service Organization set up headquarters on Eighth and K Streets and made rooms available for social gatherings, dances, and places to write letters. In the basement of the Cathedral of the Blessed Sacrament, Fathers Richard Dwyer and Vito Mistretta ran a drop-in center in the cathedral basement for Catholic military personnel. There too young people in uniform could relax, borrow from the local library, develop photographs, and write letters home. Beds were set up in the Memorial Auditorium for service people who could not find a vacancy in Sacramento hotels.

Sacramento's retailers pledge not to gouge buyers during World War II.

Wartime privations hit Sacramento as rationing and conservation became a part of home-front mobilization. Sacramento retailers gathered en masse and with hands uplifted swore not to use the war emergency as an excuse to gouge customers. Increased wartime taxes stymied spending anyway. "We couldn't sell anything during the war," complained one businessman. "The government took 85 percent of our profits for the war effort." Rubber and gasoline shortages meant fewer automobiles. Restrictions on sugar meant the substitution of the gooey thick Karo syrup in candy and other sweets. Shoes were limited to three pairs per year per person. Nylon stockings, the most famous black-market item of the war years, were also in short supply in Sacramento. Sacramentans were urged to grow "victory gardens," and an annual contest sponsored by the *Sacramento Bee* awarded a prize to the best garden.

JAPANESE RELOCATION

In 1941, nearly 5,000 Japanese-Americans resided in the greater Sacramento area. The FBI had undertaken surveillance of potential German, Italian, and Japanese "fifth columnists," and although the agency reported that the Japanese were not a serious threat, anti-Japanese sentiment fostered a climate of suspicion. Sacramento's Japanese had been subjected to increasing mistrust since the beginning of the twentieth century. The Gentlemen's Agreement of 1907 began to restrict immigration from abroad, and in Sacramento anti-Japanese predilection was stirred up by Valentine McClatchy, who after a trip to the Far East early in the century returned with a deep conviction that Asians, especially Japanese, could not be assimilated. On the pages of the *Sacramento Bee*, McClatchy preached a virulent anti-Japanese message. In 1913, the California legislature passed the Alien Land Act, forbidding Japanese from owning land. Schools were also segregated.

Once war began, officials of the Western Defense Command under General John L. DeWitt pressed for evacuation and internment. On February 19, 1942, President Roosevelt signed Executive Order 9066 giving the secretary of war the authority to designate "military areas" from which "any and all persons may be excluded." General DeWitt then designated the western half of the Pacific Coast states and Arizona as military areas. These became the prohibitive zones for the Japanese. Subsequent proclamations imposed curfews and initiated the process of evacuation.

Crackdowns on Japanese Sacramentans began almost immediately. Three prominent Sacramento businessmen—Rikitaro Sato, F.J. Miyagawa, and Gichi Aoki—were arrested as enemy aliens. FBI officers swept down on the Sumitomo Bank in Sacramento, freezing its assets. Agents seized and closed Japanese-owned companies like the New Eagle Drug Company, the Highland Investment Company, and the Pacific Trading Company. Local Japanese tried to assure city leaders of their loyalty and support for the American war effort; however, in March 1942, orders came that Sacramento was in the restricted zone and that mass evacuation must begin. The evacuation started in May. The *Bee* sported banner headlines on May 7: "All Japanese Must Get Out of Sacramento." By May 13, 3,800 Japanese were bussed to an assembly point northeast of Sacramento called Walerga Alien Induction Center from buses departing from the Memorial Auditorium. Housed in primitive barracks, the Japanese waited for transportation to "secure" locations. By May 16 the evacuation to Walerga was completed. By mid-June the large group at Walerga was transported to Tule Lake, just a few miles from the Oregon border. Walerga was then transformed into a new army base named Camp Kohler.

Although internees were permitted to return after 1945, of the 6,764 Japanese citizens of the county exiled by internment, only 4,000 returned. A number simply turned their backs on California and Sacramento and relocated to other parts of the country. Historian Cheryl Cole notes, "The reception given Japanese returning to their hometown was cool. There was no welcome, no apologies, no sympathy expressed for their suffering." For those who did come back to Sacramento's Japantown, they found their homes occupied by others. Many found temporary quarters in churches until they got on their feet. Historian Wayne Maeda observes that the returning Japanese expanded the boundaries of Japantown, moving east from the original Second and Fifth, L and O Street boundary to Seventh and south to S Street. But in searching for housing, they ran into legal road blocks set up by restrictive covenants—clauses written into property transactions that barred homeowners from selling to African Americans or people of the Mongolian race. Such restrictions were ruled unconstitutional after the war. Other Japanese returnees came back to agricultural pursuits in Elk Grove, Florin, and in the Pocket area of Sacramento.

NEW DEMOGRAPHICS: THE LATINO PRESENCE

In 1940, only 2,196 Mexicans lived in Sacramento County, roughly one percent of the total population. Initially attracted by agricultural work, the first "Great Mexican Harvest" had been in 1920. Mexicans in Sacramento found employment at Southern Pacific and local canneries, especially after Congress imposed immigration restrictions on Southern and Eastern Europeans in the 1920s. Early Mexican barrios included Alkali Flat near the rail yards and across the river in Broderick and Gardenland. Clearly, the highest concentration of Mexican residents was in the West End, a section of the city richly described by Ernesto Galarza in his famous autobiographical account *Barrio Boy*. With the increase in Mexican population during and after the Second World War, Mexican residential areas began to spread south on Franklin Boulevard when immigrants from Chihuahua and Durango in Northern Mexico arrived to work in the canneries. Through the 1940s Mexicans made up 40-50 percent of all employment in Sacramento canneries. Agricultural workers strung hops vines, cut asparagus, and thinned sugar beet plants.

The growing visibility of Mexicans was perhaps first noticed by local Catholic churches, especially the cathedral where Mexican Catholics came for baptism and

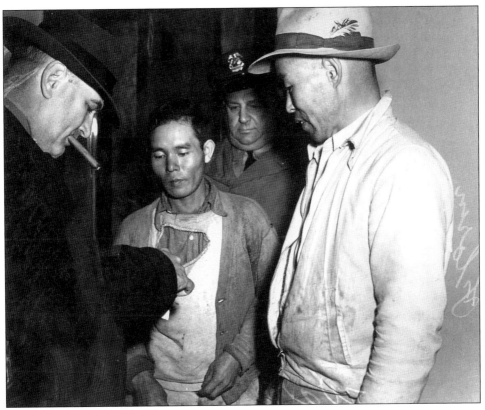

Japanese man is interrogated by police prior to internment.

weekly Mass. Likewise, the records of St. Mary's Church, then on Seventh and T, noted larger numbers of Hispanic baptisms. Already in 1919, the Ortiz family of Broderick had hosted a celebration in honor of the Mexican national icon, Our Lady of Guadalupe, on December 12 with local Catholic bishops participating in the event. In the late 1920s, Father Stephen Keating, an assistant priest at the cathedral with a background in social work, began to seek out Mexican families. Two church workers, Frederico Falcon, a native of Fresnillo, and former nun Magdalena Martinez, assisted in rounding up the scattered flock. Keating held religious services and provided instructions for Hispanics. He also collected food and clothing for them, helped them with legal problems, and sponsored social gatherings. Keating and Falcon (an accomplished musician) formed the popular Santo Nombre marching band, a Hispanic troupe that marched and played in civic parades and on different occasions. Keating's departure from the priesthood in the late 1930s left Falcon with the task of keeping the flock together.

In 1942, wartime shortages of labor compelled Congress to approve the importation of Mexican labor under the Bracero program, and Mexicans were brought north to work at the Southern Pacific yards. Hence the number of Mexicans living in the Sacramento area surged dramatically. During and after the

Mexican workers, like these at Southern Pacific, came in greater numbers during and after the Second World War (c. 1940s).

war, Mexican Sacramentans developed clusters of community. Alkali Flat continued to be "Barrio Centro," and along 12th Street a Mexican commercial district flourished with shops and various clubs like Los Reyes, La Mexicali, El San Diego, and El Xochimilco. Other cultural institutions included a Mexican Baptist church and a Methodist church. By 1944, Sacramento's Catholic Mexicans managed to raise enough money to purchase a former Catholic church on Third and O Streets that had become a Japanese theater house. Falcon and the cathedral priests opened the new church in December, naming it Our Lady of Guadalupe. This religious center provided yet another important gathering point for the Mexican citizens of Sacramento and a place to crystallize their social, religious, and cultural life. Countless fairs, dances, and religious festivals emanated from the church. In 1956, when the community had outgrown the church, the pastor petitioned for a new site at Seventh and T on property that had once housed St. Mary's Italian Church (it had moved east in 1948). The huge new church, designed by Sacramento architect Harry Devine, was dedicated in 1959. Facing Southside Park, it sported a huge mosaic of Our Lady of Guadalupe that dominated the small stretch of T Street.

THE AFRICAN-AMERICAN PRESENCE

The center of African-American cultural life was to be found at the city's two historic black churches, St. Andrew's African Methodist Episcopal Church (AME) and Siloam (after 1891 Shiloh) Baptist Church. A new church, Kyle Baptist, founded by minister Louis Harvey, added yet another center of African-American visibility. Black businesses maintained a sustaining trade in Sacramento. In 1917, George Dunlap opened the Dunlap Dining Room at 612 J Street. Its home-style cuisine attracted a diverse crowd. The restaurant later moved to Oak Park. Black journalist William Collins founded a small black newspaper, the *Western Observer*, broadcasting news of the black community. Then in 1942, a successor founded the *Sacramento Outlook*, followed by the *Sacramento Observer*, which began in 1962. Harvey and Collins also helped to found a chapter of the NAACP in 1923, and the two men took a role in blunting the influence of the Ku Klux Klan (although Klan members in a public relations stunt had ostentatiously repainted Harvey's first West End church).

Black Sacramentans fared badly in the Depression. But with the advent of the airbases, their numbers grew, reaching 1,500 by 1940. Wartime also brought additional black residents, especially military men. Racial discrimination was a fact of life in Sacramento. African Americans were not permitted to use the facilities of the YMCA or to join either the Girl or Boy Scouts. They were barred from service in other public facilities. In June 1943, 31-year-old Private Nathan Randall of McClellan was refused a drink in a bar at the Bank Café on Fourth Street. When Randall demanded service, other African Americans witnessing the event joined him and a brief scuffle with police ensued. Later, housing would continue to be an important part of the struggle for civil rights in Sacramento.

ENTERTAINMENT

Sacramento life was not always consumed during the 1930s and 1940s with the grim realities of Depression and war. Movies were still popular during the economic downturn. Feature length films, together with newsreels, shorts, and cartoons, drew Sacramentans downtown to popular movie theaters. Sacramentans could dance to the sound of the big bands at the Trianon, located above the Senator Theater, and listen to jazz at the Zanzibar Club, an African-American club that featured musical greats Duke Ellington, Count Basie, and Dinah Washington. Big band sounds also pulsed from the Memorial Auditorium as Tommy Dorsey, Benny Goodman, Glenn Miller, and Les Brown ("and his band of renown") played the sometimes mellow and sometimes animated syncopations of Swing Jazz.

The military also contributed to Sacramento's cultural life. The McClellan Band played at public concerts at Land Park. Camp Kohler hosted a popular beauty pageant and dance. But as they had in World War I, local military officials tried to curtail the activities of soldiers on liberty by urging them to stay away from gambling and prostitution. Sacramento's vice spots flourished nonetheless as illegal lotteries, illicit gambling, prostitution, and after-hours drinking took place both on the West End and across the river in nearby Broderick. Likewise, despite a presidential order outlawing prostitution near military bases, Sacramento's houses of ill repute flourished until 1943 when military commanders threatened to put the entire city off-limits unless the brothels were closed down.

Sports-minded Sacramentans got the thrill of their lives in the summer of 1942 when the local Sacramento Solons won the Pacific Coast League pennant. Professional baseball had been a popular Sacramento pastime since 1886 when the California League invited the Altas, a local team, to join the new professional circuit. The Altas, later renamed the Senators, were a popular sensation, packing in crowds at a stadium at Snowflake Park. A new team, the Gilt Edge, succeeded the Senators in 1898. In 1905, the recently formed Pacific Coast League franchise from Tacoma moved to Sacramento. In 1910, the team moved to a new ballpark at Riverside and Broadway, known over the years as Buffalo Park. In 1922, the 10,000 seat Moreing Field (named for owner Lew Moreing) replaced Buffalo Park's wooden grandstand and bleachers. The field, once acclaimed as one of the finest in the West, was subsequently renamed Cardinal Field, Doubleday Park, and finally, to honor a local sportswriter, Edmonds Field. The team was acquired in 1935 by businessman Branch Rickey, general manager of the St. Louis Cardinals who made Sacramento the Cardinal's tenth farm club. He renamed the park Cardinal Field and the team became known as the Solons. The Solons had a difficult time securing the pennant—at one point forcing a change in league rules

Edmonds Field was home to the Sacramento Solons, who won the Pacific Coast pennant in 1942.

that awarded the prize only to those who had won the most games instead of the all important play-offs. In September 1942, over 11,000 crammed into the newly-renamed Edmonds Field to watch pitcher Tony Freitas hurl a four hitter to defeat the Los Angeles Angels and clinch the first and only pennant the Solons won. Later, however, they lost the league play-offs to Seattle and the next year fell into a disappointing last place. In July 1948, the old wooden Edmonds Field burned to the ground and a new (and aesthetically less satisfying) stadium took its place. When the team departed for Hawaii in 1960, the field was demolished. A brief revival of the Solons took place between 1974 and 1976, but for a time the city appeared to have lost interest.

THE END OF THE WAR

Few Sacramentans took to the streets when Hitler's Germany finally surrendered in May 1945. Stores remained open, workers at their desks, and children in school. At McClellan Field, Mather, the Army Signal Depot, and Camp Kohler it was "just another day." Ongoing coverage of the bloody Pacific theater vied with local news. Indeed, the headline story of the atomic bombing of Hiroshima shared the spotlight with the death of longtime U.S. Senator and Sacramento native Hiram Johnson. Editorial writer Walter Jones of the *Sacramento Bee* warned, "Atomic power must not become a Frankenstein monster to America whose scientists played such a major role in the production of this terrifying instrument of war." But few appeared to be worried about the implications of the giant mushroom cloud. Sacramento was still insulated from most international trends.

But eventually Sacramento burst the bonds of its public reserve. On the afternoon of August 14, 1945, the wait ended. Anxious but subdued crowds began to congregate on K Street in anticipation of President Truman's 4 p.m. address formally announcing the end of the conflict. (Worried police Chief Alec McAllister had banned liquor sales—a fruitless effort as subsequent events revealed.) As soon as Truman's nasally Missouri twang announced the end of the Japanese war, the city erupted in celebratory chaos. The main thoroughfare of K Street became a parking lot as horns blared, whistles shrieked, firecrackers popped, and crowds surged into the streets. At Tenth and K, sailors tried to direct snarled traffic, contributing to the confusion. Overhead, a huge four-motored bomber twisted and dipped as it buzzed over the city again and again. "Even the roar of its great motors were drowned by the tumult," reported a jubilant *Sacramento Bee*. Less obtrusively but still near the center of action, worshippers, some of them dabbing tears from their eyes, went in and out of the Cathedral of the Blessed Sacrament at 11th and K, "giving thanks to Him that the war was at an end." An old era closed for Sacramento.

6. THE EMERGENCE OF A METROPOLIS

In early 1942, the Chamber of Commerce, encouraged by the economic vitality pumped into Sacramento by the military installations, laid out an ambitious program to enhance Sacramento as a commercial and population center for Northern California. City futurists envisioned Sacramento in the far-off year of 2000 as a city with anywhere between 400,000 to 800,000 people and of thousands of square acres coming from fresh annexations. The Chamber prophesied a city skyline in which "a half dozen more office buildings from fourteen to twenty stories" would dwarf the stately Elks Temple, the Cathedral of the Blessed Sacrament, the capitol building, and the California Western Life Insurance Company building. The Sacramento of 2000 would have solved its growing traffic problems and increased its economic prosperity. And above all she would keep her trees. The report predicted: "For Sacramento, in her march to metropolitan greatness, has not sacrificed the shade trees for which she was renowned so widely back in 1942."

Amazingly, many of the prognostications proved true. The Sacramento of 2000 in fact has surpassed the 400,000 population mark and annexations have augmented the city. New buildings indeed dwarf the cathedral and the Elks Temple. Through reliance on federal and state dollars and employment, the city did grow significantly, especially in undeveloped hinterlands of Sacramento County. As in most communities in the nation, Sacramento coped with the reality of a deteriorating downtown and also with the demands of a mass consumption culture that transformed it dramatically.

NEW URBAN LEADERS

The reign of longtime Mayor Thomas Monk (city leader since 1938) came to an end in 1945. Among those who later held the office were funeral home director George L. Klumpp and Sacramento City College dean Belle Cooledge, who was the city's first female mayor. The more powerful position, however, continued to be the city manager. Since 1930, architect James S. Dean had held the post. When

Dean departed for a state job in 1943, Elton Sherwin briefly held the post until his death in 1946 brought about the appointment of 42-year-old Bartley Cavanaugh. The namesake and son of a famous Sacramento city politician of earlier years, Cavanaugh remained in the office until 1964. Besides having a common touch and unusual political skills, Cavanaugh was an important force in responding to the challenges of the postwar era.

Cavanaugh shook up the lethargic city government, firing the chief of police and several police captains. He aggressively pursued new business and infrastructure improvements. Between 1946 and 1955, the city annexed 27 districts and increased its size by nearly 10 square miles. Unoccupied areas, like River Park, came into the city limits without too many difficulties. Annexation strategies took organizers first to the less-affluent south area suburbs. In early 1948, elections were scheduled for Colonial Heights, Fruitridge, and Coloma Heights. However, in these populated areas, the annexation movement took place more slowly. Many residents of Sacramento's borderlands who feared higher taxes and less control were lukewarm at best to the prospect of annexation.

City manager Bartley Cavanaugh Jr. aggressively pursued new business and infrastructure improvements.

McClellan Air Force Base was once one of the best-equipped supply and aircraft maintenance bases in the nation, shown here in 1948.

The Colonial Heights-Fruitridge opponents filed court appeals to block the elections, but elections moved forward. Coloma Heights only agreed to join the city after a deal was struck over who would assume the community's heavy bonded indebtedness. Annexation was slowed further when the vote for Sutterville Heights failed narrowly in late 1947. Despite the fact that more south area communities were added in the early 1950s, annexation proponents were dealt a big blow when affluent Arden Arcade refused to join the city in a decisive vote in 1959. The last big annexation battle was over North Sacramento, a town that once dreamed of being a city in its own right. After earlier failed votes, North Sacramento voted narrowly to join Sacramento in 1964. By this time, the once strong proponents of annexation began to change their minds as the merits of taking in less developed and poorer districts became problematic.

ECONOMIC EXPANSION: GOVERNMENT AND PRIVATE SECTORS

Cavanaugh and others were caught in a whirlwind of growth and change after World War II. Important modifications in government policies delivered the national economy from revisiting the economic morass of the Great Depression. In particular, government sponsorship of higher education for returning G.I.s and substantial subsidies and incentives for independent home-ownership helped to transform the social landscape of America. Sacramento in particular benefited from the massive expenditures for military and defense related products. Increases in the defense budget was the wind in Sacramento's economic sails during the postwar era. Expanded employment opportunities generated by federal military installations, burgeoning state and local governments, and private enterprise created a new economic climate in Sacramento. The jobs generated by these not only produced new wealth, but also rearranged population centers.

The three military installations—McClellan, Mather, and the Army Signal Depot—provided the majority of employment. McClellan was the flagship. When Cold War tensions rose after World War II, the base buzzed with life. By 1952, it employed more than 17,000 (most of them civilians and 20 percent of them women), and the numbers grew steadily, hitting a peak of 25,900 in 1968. The government poured in hundreds of millions of dollars to expand and upgrade the base over the years. By 1955, its $72 million payroll was the largest in Sacramento County. Two years earlier the *Sacramento Bee* noted that base employees made local purchases of around $14 million.

Similar increases took place in the local, state, and federal government workforce. Since the 1920s, the presence of state government had been growing. Sacramento legislators had made repeated efforts to end the evil of "scatteration" (i.e., the diffusion of state offices to different locations, especially San Francisco) and by the end of World War II had had some success. Sacramento made important improvements for the legislators, such as the introduction of air conditioning and successful mosquito abatement programs. But more than anything else, the rapid postwar growth in California required a growing, full-time government. Governor Edmund G. Brown reorganized the executive branch in the early 1960s, creating centralized departments. Jess Unruh, a Los Angeles assemblyman, helped expand and modernize the state legislature. In 1966, voters approved Proposition 1A, which created a full-time legislature. This retooled government required more workers and specialists, and they usually lived in Sacramento.

Even before Proposition 1A, city life quickened as more bureaucrats were hired to staff the increasing number of state agencies. Lobbyists, legislators, and other hangers-on frequented the fading Senator Hotel. Here in the 1940s and early 1950s reigned the "uncrowned king" of the legislature, Artie Samish, who was the lobbyist for the truck and bus lines, the liquor companies, and the race tracks. An expose by *Collier's* magazine spelled the decline of his influence, and in 1953 he was "dethroned" by a conviction for federal income tax evasion. Sacramento became more of a government town than it had ever been. Between the air bases and government employment, Sacramento's traditional reliance on the rail yards, retailing, and agricultural production faded. By 1956, state Director of Industrial Relations Ernest B. Webb noted that government units employed 40 percent of all non-farm workers in Sacramento, far outstripping the rest of the state where government workers made up only 17 percent of the non-farm total.

City and county governments worked closely with the Chamber of Commerce to attract new businesses. One of the biggest coups was snaring a share of the growing aerospace industry that came to California after the war. A Christmastime 1950 headline in the *Sacramento Bee*, "Rocket Plants to be Erected East of Capital," announced the arrival of Aerojet General Corporation, a subsidiary of General Tire and Rubber. The aerospace giant that made rocket engines for the federal government secured a 7,200-acre tract 16 miles east of the city. Paying a whopping $6.6 million for the new plant, Aerojet peaked in 1963, giving paychecks to 19,792 employees and accounting for more than 60 percent of the region's manufacturing employment. Aerojet was but one of a number of private companies that discovered the cheap land, abundant power sources, and friendly business climate of Sacramento County. In 1956, Aerojet sold 2,000 acres of its vast holdings to the Douglas Aircraft Company, which also began missile testing.

While the aerospace acquisitions were the big prize, other private firms came as well. By 1948, the city had an "industrial park" on Richards Boulevard. Its occupants included paper giant Crown Zellerbach, which opened in July 1949. In May 1951, Procter & Gamble, the Cincinnati-based soap king, opened a plant on Power Inn Road. Other firms like Federal Mogul, a ball-bearing manufacturer, Firestone Tire, and Campbell Soup all relocated to prime sites, providing hundreds of jobs and diversifying the economic profile of the community.

Aerojet General, a subsidiary of General Tire and Rubber, sets off a couple of its rockets.

POPULATION GROWTH

The lure of jobs caused Sacramento's population to skyrocket. The location of job centers outside the city shifted the demographic center to the heretofore-undeveloped lands of the county. In 1940, 62 percent of county residents lived in the city and 38 percent in the county. In 1950, the scales balanced evenly with 50 percent in the city and 50 percent in the county. However, by 1960 the percentage of city to county dwellers flipped exactly from the numbers of 1940 with 62 percent residing in the county and 38 percent in the city.

Year	1940	1950	1960
City Population	105,958	137,572	191,667
% Growth from Prev. Decade	13%	30%	39%
County Population	64,375	139,568	311,111
% Growth from Prev. Decade	33%	117%	123%

Source: Sacramento Archives and Museum Collection Center

Much of this growth continued to be focused on the northeast corridor extending out along Highway 40, Auburn Boulevard, and Fair Oaks Boulevard. However, in the south area of Stockton Boulevard, Franklin, and Freeport, expansion continued as well, stretching until it touched the tip of rural Elk Grove and began to draw rural Galt into its swirl.

SACRAMENTO'S NEW SUBURBS

Before the war, few Sacramentans lived more than three or four blocks from the streetcar tracks, but new industries, new freeways, and automobility allowed Sacramentans to empty out into the suburbs. In some instances, growth occurred in existing settlements. The area immediately around McClellan Field moved swiftly to take advantage of the opening of the base. "Come to North Sacramento, Hagginwood and Del Paso Heights," ran one newspaper ad. "The Giant $7,000,000 Army Air Depot Insures Rapid But Solid Development of the District!" In fact, Del Paso Heights grew so rapidly that by 1955 local citizens were pushing for incorporation as a sixth class city. Military bases themselves built government housing for base residents. McClellan's Capeheart community and the Wherry Homes of Mather provided neat residential enclaves for on-base personnel. Likewise, older communities like Carmichael, Fair Oaks, Orangevale, and Florin, which had enjoyed a rather sleepy semi-rural existence, burst into life as developers turned over fields, knocked down orchards, and built new homes.

Whole new colonies sprang up as well. McClellan Air Force Base stimulated the growth northeast of the city and north of the American River (one subdivision was named "Aerohaven"). Flagship developments of the suburban frontier included River Park and Arden Park that filled with ranch-style homes and

119

upwardly mobile, white middle-class inhabitants. Developer Jere Strizek would capitalize on the rapid growth of McClellan by creating a whole new suburb: North Highlands, a concentrated image of Sacramento's suburban growth. With the encouragement of base commanders, Strizek purchased a 2,000-acre tract near McClellan in 1950 and began building. At its peak, Strizek's workers were churning out a new home every 12 hours. North Highlands skyrocketed from about 150 people in 1951 to over 22,000 eight years later.

To the south of the city, the construction of the U.S. Army Signal Depot and the opening of the Campbell Soup Plant brought working-class subdivisions called Hollywood Park, Sutterville Heights, and Freeport Village. Along Florin Road, housing tracts, service stations, and supermarkets began to pop up like dandelions. Parkway Estates began in the 1950s, advertising their tract homes with promises of freeway proximity and assuring slogans, "Quality is not expensive." Virtually all of these new homes were eligible for FHA loans.

New Schools

Into these new colonies were also inserted schools. The growth in Sacramento's young reflected national baby-boom trends and consequently an increasing demand for schools. Since the late 1940s, voters had passed bond issues to improve the aging grade schools and the two city high schools. Burgeoning baby boomers taxed existing school facilities. By 1949–1950, the enrollment of Sacramento's schools spiked over 30,000. In May 1951, voters approved a $6.5 million bond issue and a 50¢ increase in taxes to provide funds for new schools and additions to others. By the 100th anniversary of the Sacramento City Unified School District in 1954, there were twenty-four elementary schools, five junior highs, two senior high schools, a junior college, and a highly successful adult education program. New Sacramento high schools opened, including Hiram Johnson in 1959, Luther Burbank in 1962, and John F. Kennedy High in 1967.

Sacramento also finally received a four-year institution of higher learning in 1947. Postwar needs for teachers and an expanding educational system provided an opening for State Senator Earl Desmond to propose the formation of a new branch of the network of state teacher's colleges that already dotted the state. After much debate, the legislature approved the establishment of the new college and appointed former Chico professor Guy L. West as the first president of what would become known as "Sac State."

The college began in the buildings of the City College while the campus was being built on former farming lands near the growing River Park subdivision. This small "academic village" grew rapidly and became an important asset as its programs began to enrich cultural life. In addition to teaching duties, the faculty provided a cadre of experts for local media and other state and city needs. The schools of engineering and education poured their graduates into local businesses and schools. The university's trained historians provided some of the resources used to write this history. Sac State professors V. Aubrey Neasham and Joseph

California State University, Sacramento, shown here in March 1957, became an important cultural asset as its programs began to enrich cultural life.

McGowan spearheaded the research that undergirded the restoration of "Old Sacramento" and explored other areas of local development. An array of local politicians came from Sacramento State, including Mayor Joe Serna Jr. and Grantland Johnson, a city councilman and state official. Concerts, dance recitals, and art exhibits found a showcase at the college. Public radio broadcasting from the campus began in 1964 with a 10-watt transmitter under the title KERS. Gradually expanding its wattage and scope, the station eventually became KXPR, a classical music station with programming in public affairs and a late-night jazz program.

With the formation of American River Junior College in 1955, yet another outlet for college-bound Sacramentans was available. Setting up its location in suburban Carmichael, the junior college became a magnet for suburban youth who took their first two years of general education before moving on to the state college or university system. The Los Rios Community College District took Sacramento City College out of the city school district and began a network of two year colleges that absorbed American River College. In 1961, a master plan for higher education was devised by the education-friendly administration of Governor Edmund G. "Pat" Brown (1958–1966) that brought additional resources and upgrading to Sacramento's college system. In 1972, Sacramento State was incorporated into the larger state university system and became known as California State University at Sacramento.

INFRASTRUCTURE: A NEW SYSTEM OF ROADS AND FREEWAYS

Sacramento's love affair with the automobile became permanent in the postwar era, and the proliferation of cars soon affected the quality of life downtown. Public transit began to evaporate. The venerable streetcar made its exit in the late 1940s when PG&E sold its long-held franchise to the National City Lines. This large company, a front for auto, bus, and tire companies, specialized in replacing streetcars with more efficient buses, and in 1947 Sacramento's last streetcar service shut down. Eventually, the bus lines would be transferred to city ownership since private businesses could no longer make a profit on a service that was largely replaced by independent automobile ownership. With the proliferation of cars, city officials worried openly that Sacramento would suffer if there were not adequate provisions, so they quickly approved the construction of a 1,400-space parking garage on an entire city block north of I Street in the 1950s.

Dependence on the automobile was further enhanced by the development of the freeway system. The route of U.S. 40, the main continental freeway, ran through the state capital over the Tower Bridge and out 16th Street. In the early 1940s, the North Sacramento freeway was opened, replacing an older road that was subject to periodic water inundation. In 1947, the California Division of Highways and the U.S. Bureau of Public Roads undertook an "origin and destination" survey of the greater Sacramento area. They chronicled the increase in the volume of traffic, and by 1949, city officials tagged the traffic situation as the "number 1 problem" affecting the area's future. An extensive survey revealed that nearly 350,000 automobile trips were generated daily, 84 percent of which were within the county. Plotting a new freeway plan in 1950, engineers went to work designing a new road system around Sacramento that accommodated (and encouraged) the new automobile culture. In 1955, the construction of the "Elvas Freeway" improved traffic flow to the northeast corner of the city. The plan expanded in 1955 to include the southeast corner of the city in a section known as the 29th and 30th Street Freeway, which also included a new span across the American River.

The enactment of the 1957 National Defense Highway Act provided additional funds to connect California with the nationwide interstate system. Preparations for the Winter Olympics at Squaw Valley in 1960 hastened the development of Interstate 80, which followed the old Southern Pacific route eastward over Donner Pass, overtaking the old Highway 40. Sacramentans now had free access to Reno and Carson City. Interstate 80 continued with a spur across the old city limits and East Sacramento along 30th Street. Ribbons of concrete went down across the city along 29th and 30th Streets and another at W and X Streets. A new bridge spanned the Sacramento River joining the W-X Street Freeway with Yolo County.

Modernization of Highway 50 extended Sacramento's reach beyond the confines of Folsom Road and Fair Oaks Boulevard and proceeded outward toward Folsom and into the foothills. To the south the widening and expansion of and rerouting of Highway 99 from Stockton Boulevard knitted the rapidly developing south area even more firmly to the wider metropolitan area. The extension of Interstate 5, a roadway that runs the full length of the state, was delayed in Sacramento due to routing difficulties. But once it was complete, all roads converged on the state capital as a spaghetti bowl of freeway interchanges and off-ramps reconfigured venerable neighborhoods, created and destroyed businesses, and reinforced Sacramento's dependence on the automobile.

AIR TRANSPORT AND A DEEP-WATER PORT

Adding to the transportation revolution in the city were two major developments: a new airport and a deep water port. The need for improved air transportation systems also pressed hard. Sacramento's municipal airport (Metropolitan Field) came into being in 1931 off Freeport Boulevard. It had three runways, and its main commercial carrier was Boeing Airways, later consolidated into United Airlines. The airport grew steadily throughout the 1930s and 1940s, fortified by government airmail service.

In 1958, a joint city-county committee contracted with the airport consultation firm of Leigh Fisher & Associates. A year later, Fisher submitted a report calling for a new airport to serve the growing area. The most controversial aspect of the report called for relocation. In spite of criticism, the board went forward and

The expansion of Interstate 5, shown here near Second and Third Streets in May 1968, was delayed because of routing difficulties but once completed conributed to the reconfiguration of the city.

123

selected a site in the North Natomas area 12 miles northwest of the capital along I-5. With the help of effective lobbying by Congressman John E. Moss and city officials, ground was broken in 1964. By late fall of 1967, a proud Moss appeared at the dedication of the new $22 million Sacramento Metropolitan Field (later renamed Sacramento International Airport). Under the direction of James Carr, the airport expanded to receive jumbo jets.

The desire to make Sacramento a deep-water port went back to the Progressive era. The prospect of using the river as a commercial artery again became possible after hydraulic mining ended and the possibility of keeping the channel clear enough to receive sailing vessels re-emerged. Federal dollars pursued by area congressmen brought about navigation improvements, and the City built new wharves and terminals. Over 5,000 tons of freight and 840 tons of rice grown in the region's wetlands were shipped through Sacramento in the 1930s. Legislators managed to create a joint Sacramento/Yolo Port District in the 1930s, but it was not until mid-1945 that the Army Corps of Engineers signed off on the construction of a deep channel to connect Sacramento with the Bay Area. In July 1946, President Harry Truman approved the plan, and on August 7, 1949, groundbreaking took place.

Although delayed by the Korean War and problems with funding, the project went slowly forward, pushed every step of the way by Congressman Moss. Despite further delays due to Sacramento's silty river bottom, the port welcomed its first visitor in June 1963, the 8,000 ton Taiwanese freighter S.S. *Taipei Victory*, whose cargo hull was filled with Sacramento area rice. The port never materialized as its advocates predicted. Strong competition from the nearby Port of Stockton along with continued problems keeping the channel of the Sacramento River clean have hampered its potential.

WATER PROJECTS AND NEW POWER

A long delayed Folsom Dam was completed in 1955 and with it the accompanying Nimbus spill-off. Like the port, efforts for damming the American River had been in the works since after World War I. In 1946, Folsom incorporated as a city and plans were laid for the construction of a new dam and additional hydroelectric generation. By the early 1950s, in the wake of the need to prevent floods, promote recreation, and meet the electrical needs of Sacramento businesses, as well as the growing number of "all electric" homes, federal monies flowed into Folsom. In 1956, the new structure was dedicated after having already proven its worth in the wet winter of 1955 when it held back the waters of a swollen American River in one of the worst flooding seasons the region would see until the inundation of 1985–1986. In 1955, SMUD was approved for a generation plant on the American River, and in 1961 kilowatt hours began pumping from the new facility. The dam also created Folsom Lake, a popular recreation spot, and Lake Natoma, which sits below the bluffs of suburban Orangevale. In another development, the long-stalled plans to transform the banks of the American River into a jogging and

The Taipei Victory *arrived at the Port of Sacramento on June 29, 1963.*

recreational trail materialized in the 1970s. Stretching 23 miles from Hazel Avenue and the Nimbus Fish Hatchery, west to Discovery Park at the confluence of the American and Sacramento Rivers, joggers, naturalists, and rafters flocked to the trail, making it one of the most popular recreation sites in the area.

HEALTH CARE

Sacramento desperately needed more modern health care facilities. Area hospitals, benefiting from federal loans and grants under the Hill-Burton Act of 1949, applied for and received substantial aid to expand their facilities and improve their technology. A massive building project at the County Hospital in the early 1950s added over 400 beds. Likewise, private health care centers like Sutter and Mercy General Hospitals also expanded. Maternity wards in both were booming during these years, and the general increase in children pressed the Sisters of Mercy to convert their old nursing school (it had closed in 1950) into a children's hospital. In addition, the Episcopal Church erected the million-dollar St. Luke Medical Center on Capitol Avenue. Scores of new office buildings housed clinics for a variety of health care professionals, including the growing number of pediatricians, orthodontists, and optometrists. In response to federal initiatives,

125

Efforts to dam the American River had been in the works since after World War I.

the University of California at Davis Medical School made the Sacramento County Hospital its teaching hospital in 1966. In 1973, the school purchased the hospital outright. Renamed the U.C. Davis Medical Center in 1978, the hospital serves as a teaching facility for physicians in training as well as expanding the scope of services and therapies for the region. In 1965, Kaiser-Permanente health care came to Sacramento and opened a facility on Morse Avenue. Secured by lucrative contracts with local federal employees, Kaiser provides pre-paid health care benefits for scores of Sacramentans.

REDEVELOPMENT

New residents, as well as city families, poured into the suburbs, thereby decreasing the city's tax base and leaving behind the maintenance and upgrading of its infrastructure. Urban churches lost congregations, stores closed, and even the lure of movies and other cultural events at downtown theaters and the Memorial Auditorium became less and less attractive. Many of the questions about the downtown's future focused on the deteriorating buildings of the West End, whose boundaries though somewhat fluid stretched from the river east to Seventh Street and south of the Southern Pacific Depot to R or S Street.

Sacramentans held two different images of the West End. Suburban developers, politicians, and newcomers accustomed to small-town life viewed it as a cauldron of urban pathologies. It had lots of bars, fast food joints, flop houses, employment agencies, and houses of ill-repute. It also had a very low tax base, yet consumed the lion's share of expenditures for fire and police calls. The residential structures of the district were not only a public relations liability, but also a public health hazard. Absentee landlords owned over 80 percent of its buildings. In a series of articles in 1949, *Sacramento Bee* reporter Hale Champion painted the area in the darkest possible hues. Another writer depicted the area as "the worst skid row west of Chicago."

Other Sacramentans had a different perspective. No one denied the physical deterioration of the buildings and the prevalence of crime; however, they also noted that despite its rough character, the West End provided affordable housing for nearly 10,000 transients—mostly men over the age of 55, pensioners, people of color, and other minorities. There were also businesses and entertainment venues that catered to city clientele. The West End functioned as a labor market for those who needed cheap workers for the canneries, the fields, and other assorted jobs. Some saw it as one of the last bastions of the vibrant ethnic cultures that co-existed for generations within blocks of each other in Sacramento. Within its boundaries were ethnic clubs, social halls, and remnants of Sacramento's past.

Already during the Great Depression, the federal government had begun taking a more active role in urban affairs. After the war, the commitment of the central and state governments to urban rejuvenation grew stronger. The first steps in doing something about Sacramento's rapidly decaying West End were modest. When the California Redevelopment Act, which provided state funds for local improvement projects, passed in 1945, the Sacramento City Council studied possible options for redevelopment. In October 1947, it voted to widen the parkway between the state capitol and the Tower Bridge to remove unsightly buildings and give those entering the city an uninhibited view of the seat of California's government.

Little changed until 1949 when Congress passed the Federal Housing Act. This sweeping legislation promised government subsidies not only for slum clearance but also for the construction of public housing for the displaced. Sacramento already had two public housing projects, New Helvetia on Broadway and Dos Rios off North B Street.

The nexus of slum clearance and relocation needs would complicate redevelopment issues for years. In December of 1950, the city released its first detailed redevelopment plan. Crafted by architects Richard Neutra and Robert Alexander, it proposed an extensive program of slum removal and the construction of high rise public housing facilities interspersed among new buildings in the redevelopment zones. The Sacramento Redevelopment Agency was formed to implement this plan under the leadership of Joseph T. Bill. Studies progressed throughout the 1950s with developers identifying 233 blocks in need of transformation. However, opposition from businessmen and others to the public housing aspects of the plan mounted throughout 1951 and 1952. One way that Bill and others found to evade the requirement to relocate those who had lived in a redevelopment area for at least a year was to insist that the law's provisions only applied to families. This immediately reduced the number eligible for relocation significantly by leaving out the largest single group of denizens of the area: single men. Meanwhile, the plan stalled and was tabled in May 1953.

In the meantime, a new Republican administration had taken over in Washington, D.C. that backed away from earlier plans linking redevelopment with public housing. In July 1954, San Francisco developer Ben Swig offered a fresh plan that focused almost entirely on new shopping and business buildings in the redevelopment area. At the heart of the Swig Plan was a new K Street pedestrian mall, with moving sidewalks, that spanned from Second Street to 12th. Opponents of Swig's plan noted that it made little mention of public housing and relocation. Anger at the destruction of their property prompted West End residents to resist change and stall a ballot measure (Proposition B) in 1956 that would have enabled the city to borrow money to proceed with demolition. The Proposition B defeat, however, was only temporary. Undeterred, city leaders found other sources of financing and demolition plans proceeded, targeting the area directly in front of the state capitol as the first site for rehabilitation.

In 1957, Governor Goodwin Knight presided at the symbolic wrecking of a dilapidated Victorian on Sixth and Capitol, commencing a process that continued into the 1960s. Demolition proceeded rapidly and before long a new Capitol Mall

Sacramento redevelopment left large vacant city blocks for years until development projects became final.

emerged, providing a sweeping open space between the Tower Bridge and the statehouse. As one *Sacramento Union* columnist put it: "Where honky-tonks and gas stations once stood, a thoroughly businesslike Capitol Mall sprouted, an appropriate gateway to the Capital." In 1960, yet another plan laid out an ambitious agenda for the next phase of urban renewal—a pedestrian mall for K Street, a convention center across from the aging Memorial Auditorium, and a new historic park with a "gold rush" motif called "Old Sacramento."

Redevelopment did hit bumps. Ambitious plans for ethnic "blocks" (e.g., the Hispanic Plaza de los Flores) in redevelopment failed as money and support were not sufficient. Another major controversy erupted over the placement of Interstate 5, the north/south freeway that cuts through the heart of California. The State Department of Highways floated several plans for the new link. One proposal was to locate the freeway along the river in Old Sacramento, thereby demolishing the city's historic district. Arguing forcefully in favor of this was the Macy's Company of New York, which contemplated an anchor store for a proposed new shopping mall near the river. Arguing against the riverfront freeway was a coalition of preservationists, including Eleanor McClatchy of the *Bee*. William W. Winster, dean of the School of Architecture at the University of California at Berkeley, best articulated the concerns of this group:

> It is beyond me how a city can think of routing a freeway through so important a historic quarter. A freeway is a freeway and it can be routed anywhere. Why, this is where the Argonauts landed and this was where your merchant princes planned and built the first transcontinental railroad, and this was where California was planned and governed in those first early years.

Ultimately, a compromise was reached that preserved the first three blocks of the old city and ran the freeway between Second and Third Streets with an off-ramp close enough to the proposed new Macy's.

Redevelopment again slowed to a halt in the mid-1960s as an unsteady American economy caused many early backers to withdraw. Things looked bleak until 1967 when developers formed the Downtown Plaza Properties Group, consisting of developer George McKeon, aggregate millionaire Henry Teichert, and construction mogul William Campbell who reinvigorated the plan. "Those guys were saviors," Mayor Burnett Miller later recalled. Dividing their efforts between office and retail operations, McKeon and his associates began to fill in the empty spaces of the nearly abandoned redevelopment projects.

In the mid-1960s, Mayor Walter Christiansen made plans to develop the K Street Mall. Envisioning a broad pedestrian walkway, he and city designers attempted to recreate the feel of the Sacramento River running from the mountains (the large concrete blocks in the eastern mall) to the sea (the flatter pools and grass near Seventh Street). Likewise it was hoped that retail shopping would continue. Later, these concrete piles would be derided as "tank traps."

The long-stalled Old Sacramento project got underway in the late 1960s. City officials began to look seriously at the rehabilitation of nearly 100 historic buildings. A new wave of entrepreneurship in the area began as early as 1960 when restaurateur Newton Cope restored an 1853 firehouse and opened the posh Firehouse Restaurant in the middle of the blight. The city began to clear out the last of the residents of the run-down buildings, make assessments about salvageability, and dispatch historians and others to assist in the historic reconstruction of Sacramento's past. In 1966, the National Register for Historic Places designated this district a national landmark and the state legislature declared it a state park. In all, $33 million was poured into the Old Sacramento project.

The neglected side of the story was the plight of those displaced by the demolition of the housing in the area. The City Council empaneled a Community Welfare Council consisting of local clergy and others who studied the conditions created by redevelopment. This group issued a report in 1964 noting that from 1957 to 1963, the population of single men dropped from 5,500 to 1,400. Nearly 4,000 of these men left and the redevelopment agency could account for only 555 of them. Of this group, a little over half found housing within or adjacent to the redevelopment area while the rest either moved out of town or to other places in the metropolitan area. Sacramento simply ejected these men from their midst. Some settled in other areas of the city, but many quit Sacramento, never to return.

THE CHANGING CULTURE OF SACRAMENTO

One group displaced from the West End were the nearly 2,000 African Americans living in the redevelopment area. They saw their historic churches demolished (St. Andrew's and Shiloh) and their housing and community institutions removed. The search for affordable housing was difficult. Black Sacramentans had already defined a zone for themselves near McClellan Field, where a bus shuttled them to their jobs. After redevelopment, others were scattered all over the city with relocation points in the Oak Park area (where they already had a foothold), and south in the Glen Elder and Meadowview areas. Later, clusters at Freeport Manor and in smaller residential areas near the Western Pacific rail yards and Hughes Stadium created urban space for the African-American community. Indeed, the black population was growing at this time. By the end of the 1960s, upwardly mobile African Americans were moving into suburban areas like North Highlands, Rancho Cordova, and to the Parkway-South area. In 1960, Sacramento's black population stood at 19,805 or 3.9 percent of the total county population.

Sacramento's history of racial exclusion began to be tackled in a more systematic fashion as the national civil rights movement picked up steam, and Sacramento citizens stepped forward to end long-standing practices of racial discrimination. African Americans like Frank Canson were inducted into the police force in 1947, and his wife Fannie Canson in 1948 was the first African-

American teacher in Sacramento public schools since Sarah Mildred Jones, a black principal of Fremont School at 24th and J (1894–1914).

In early 1950, black attorney Nathaniel Colley represented the growing black professional class. Colley was one of the first, in league with the revived NAACP, to challenge cases of racial discrimination in Sacramento. In 1949, he exposed police brutality against two African-American suspects who had been beaten into confessing to the robbery of a bus passenger. In one of his first cases argued for the NAACP, Colley challenged racial exclusion at the Land Park swimming pool (*Hazel Jackson v. Land Park Plunge*, 1950)—a case he won only to see the pool closed. Later, he effectively challenged racial discrimination in the River Oaks Public Housing Project (1951–1953).

Clarence Canson and Douglas Greer, African-American attorneys, ran for city council in the 1950s. Although they lost their bids, African-American political strength mustered to elect Milton McGhee to the City Council in 1967—the first black elected official in municipal office in Sacramento. A year earlier, *Ebony Magazine's Negro Handbook* had cited Sacramento as one of the "ten best cities for Negroes." The increasing prominence of statewide black office holders like Wilson Riles and Byron Rumford also enhanced the visibility of Sacramento's growing black community.

Attorneys Douglas Greer and Nathaniel Colley shake hands at the NAACP life membership banquet.

Sacramento caught the crest of the national civil rights movement, and African-American leaders participated in marches and pressured city leaders on such issues as access to housing and job opportunities. The issue of segregation in Sacramento schools was highlighted in August 1963 when the racially-mixed Stanford Junior High School burned to the ground. Minority students were then sent to previously all-white schools to create racial balance. School desegregation in the Sacramento City Unified District went forward and influenced similar policies in neighboring districts. The federal government's war on poverty provided funds and a framework for community organization among Sacramento's poor, many of whom were black. The Sacramento Area Economic Opportunity Council (SAEOC) was the recipient of funds from the federal Office of Economic Opportunity. African Americans played an important role in this organization. Through the annexation of areas like Del Paso Heights and the growing popularity of the *Sacramento Observer*, African-American visibility increased.

Toward the end of the 1960s, civil rights militancy eclipsed the legal strategies of Colley and others. Sacramento had chapters of most national civil rights organizations, such as Congress of Racial Equality (CORE), Student Non-violent Coordinating Committee (SNCC), and the NAACP. It also had branches of more militant groups such as the Black Panther Party, the Black Student Union, and the Nation of Islam. Racial tensions flared when police arrested three heavily armed members of the militant Black Panthers who had stalked into the state capitol to protest a gun control measure the legislature had approved. An October 1968 symposium at Sac State on "Racism in America" drew nearly 10,000 participants. Black Panther leader Eldridge Cleaver delivered an impassioned 75-minute speech at Hornet Stadium denouncing capitalism and oppression and tapping into the widespread anger felt by many over the death of Martin Luther King Jr. the previous April. Simmering tensions were given a voice when federal anti-poverty legislation provided for the creation of neighborhood councils and organizations. The Oak Park Neighborhood Council reflected one such umbrella group dedicated to soothing tensions, improving services, and keeping open channels of communication.

The national difficulties of the year 1968 found their way to Sacramento. For a time, trouble had been brewing in the Oak Park district and in the area around James McClatchy Park. Police and local youths had engaged in several stand-offs, but tensions had cooled. Then a fight broke out in July between a large group of black youth and an all-white baseball team playing in McClatchy Park. A second day of unrest followed. Nervously convened meetings between the Oak Park Neighborhood Organization and city officials allowed residents to air grievances. The meetings accentuated the need for activities to undercut further violence. Recreational and neighborhood revitalization projects were launched; educational workshops, meal programs, and musical groups helped to siphon off ill will. However, efforts fell short when in the summer of 1969 gunfire erupted near the park between residents and police. The night of June 16 saw nearly 100 shots fired between police and snipers. Injuries to police and rioters resulted in 38 arrests and calls for an investigation of conditions in the deteriorating Oak Park area—as well as into the behavior of the police.

While conflict between African Americans and police continued into the 1970s, historian Clarence Cesar notes the rising economic and political clout of Sacramento's African-American community. Community leaders Rosenwald "Robbie" Robinson and Callie Carney served terms on the City Council. African Americans took prominent roles in various school boards of the area. Representation in the judiciary was increased as well. In 1975, Sacramento native William K. Morgan (owner of the Morgan-Jones Funeral Home) was appointed to the Superior Court.

MASS CONSUMPTION CULTURE

Although Sacramentans had long been a community of shoppers and frequented the well developed commercial districts along J and K Streets, in the postwar era, the culture of consumerism surged more powerfully than ever. Sacramentans joined their fellow Americans in enshrining mass consumption as a defining characteristic of U.S. culture. Historian Lizabeth Cohen has described the rise of this phenomenon in the postwar era. Government programs encouraged better education for higher paying jobs, underwrote home ownership, and expanded automobile ownership. Shopping, buying, and consuming defined local culture as never before. The shopping center emerged as the most powerful visible symbol of this new way of life.

Smaller retailing outlets like the Hollywood Mall and Arden Town led the way. In 1946, developer Jere Strizek built the first major shopping mall in Sacramento County: Town & Country. This simple shopping center was constructed with surplus materials and affected an "Old West" mystique with its use of wagon wheels and hitching rails. Town & Country's 46 stores and nearby theater were a fabulous success. In 1951, developer James Cordano worked with the Blumenfeld family to open Sacramento's first regional shopping center called Country Club Center. Anchored by J.C. Penney and Rhodes (another department store), it took root in an already rapidly growing area. The remaining lands soon filled in with tract homes, stores, and churches. Set off by an enormous parking lot, ringed with palm trees, Country Club was a smashing success. By December 1955, nearly 2,000 businesses did a healthy trade in the new shopping areas. Another rival, Arden Fair, joined the fray in 1957 and all continued to flourish in the 1960s. In the south area, Cordano developed Southgate Shopping Center in 1960, and later Sacramento's first enclosed and air-conditioned mall, Florin Center, opened in 1967. Subsequent mall development in Citrus Heights and Roseville further decentralized Sacramento's shopping experiences.

The modern supermarket made its appearance in Sacramento, displacing small retail grocery operations like those of the Arata brothers or butchers like Moehring and Yorke. Grocery chains became popular after the war, bringing all of these various food buying operations under one roof and surrounding them with capacious parking lots. Some of Sacramento's supermarkets evolved from small "mom and pop" operations. Such was the case with the Kassis brothers, a Lebanese family who came to Sacramento in the 1920s. Under the leadership of the family patriarch, A.G. Kassis, the sons began their successful business with a fruit stand on 28th and Broadway. Later, their enterprise expanded into a network of 12 stores that they christened "Stop 'n Shop," and they effectively marketed themselves with the help of a popular radio jingle.

The Kassis brothers' competitors included another family chain, lead by the Inks brothers—Charles, Russell, and Dick—who began a grocery business in 1925. Adapting new supermarket retailing techniques, the brothers forged a grocery empire of 33 supermarkets, 29 of them in the Sacramento area. Contributing to their success was their ability to move into the rapidly growing suburbs.

The popular Raley's Markets were the brainchild of Thomas Raley, who had come to California from Arkansas in 1925. He took his apprenticeship in the grocery business in the Bay Area, and in 1935 opened a small store in Placerville. In 1938, he opened his first Sacramento store on Stockton Boulevard. By 1953, he owned seven stores. Raley's eventually became the largest locally owned grocery operation in the Sacramento area. Other chains came. Lucky's opened its first market on 30th and Broadway in March 1948. The next year, florist Bert Geisreiter sold Margaret Crocker's Conservatory across from the city cemetery to the Safeway chain.

Independent grocery retailing persisted in Sacramento largely through Chinese family markets. Historian Alfred Yee has chronicled the rise and decline of locally run Chinese markets like Giant Foods and Farmer's Market, which opened in the 1930s. Belair, begun by the Wong Family as a fruit stand in rural Penryn in 1956,

Town & Country Shopping Center opened in 1946.

The Kassis brothers owned the Stop 'n Shop grocery chain.

grew dramatically as well. Ultimately these family-owned markets were gobbled up by chains such as Raley's.

Popular restaurants contributed to Sacramento's culture of mass consumption. As prosperity spread, Sacramentans began to eat meals away from home and an active restaurant industry scrambled to accommodate the new tastes. Sacramento had its revered old restaurants, like the Rosemont Grill at Ninth and J, and Posey's Cottage (a favorite spot for Governor Ronald Reagan) on Tenth and O. Frank Fat's popular Chinese eatery on L Street was also a hang-out of the political classes. More upscale dining was available at the Firehouse Restaurant in Old Sacramento. Suburban dwellers found a good venue at Aldo's Restaurant located in the Town & Country shopping center.

Sacramento also had it share of the old fashioned diners and quick lunch places typical of many cities. Stan's Drive-Ins, run by proprietor Stanley Burke, began in Sacramento in 1933. These first drive-in restaurants sported a modern design and service to the car. The huge sloppy hamburgers made at Jim Denny's on Terminal Way and 12th Street still attracts a non-stop lunch crowd. Likewise the popular Sam's Hof Brau on J Street featured piled high sandwiches served in a traditional "gasthaus" atmosphere. Vic's ice cream parlor, established in 1949 by Vic Vito and Ash Rutledge at Riverside and Eighth Avenue, perpetuated an old fashioned soda parlor ambience. Merlino's orange freeze, hawked in an orange-shaped kiosk, was a popular summer beverage.

But the real growth was in the mass produced fast-food industry that took off in Sacramento like a rocket. Fosters Freeze, a popular fast-food chain, came to Sacramento after the war and featured soft-served ice milk, fried hamburgers, and French fries. Hart's Hamburgers on Freeport Boulevard featured a neon Highlander doing a flashing light "fling." The most successful innovation in fast-food came when the McDonald's hamburger kingdom came to Sacramento in February 1954 and opened a stand on Fruitridge Boulevard. Sherwood "Shakey"

The fast-food industry took off quickly in Sacramento with places like Shakey's Pizza Parlor doing a brisk business.

Johnson and his associates are credited with popularizing pizza around the Sacramento area. The popular Shakey's Pizza shops included low-cost food, beer, and occasional entertainment by local bands.

THE NEW STATE FAIRGROUNDS

Everything changed in Sacramento in the postwar era—even the location of the state fair. Since 1906, the fairgrounds had been located on Stockton Boulevard. With the proliferation of automobile ownership, the area around the fairgrounds grew cramped and congested as local residents rented their driveways and front lawns to desperate motorists. Likewise, the aging buildings of the site began to feel their limitations. State Senator Earl Desmond proposed relocation to a new site on former grazing lands of the Swanston meat-packing company (closed since 1949) near Arden Fair. Claimed under the power of eminent domain by the State of California, the site was soon being studied by planners recruited from the Disney Corporation in Southern California to design the new exposition park. The result was a huge new concrete center surrounded by a mammoth parking lot and named the modernistic-sounding "Cal Expo." In 1967, Governor Ronald Reagan formally dedicated the site, and the old fairgrounds passed into mythic memory. The huge Golden Bears that had greeted fair-goers at the old site were transferred to Cal Expo, but seemed dwarfed by its concrete structures. It would take time for Sacramentans to warm up to the new site.

ENTERTAINMENT

If Sacramentans found common ground in shopping malls and supermarket chains, movies and television provided even more common culture. Virtually everyone in Sacramento (and in America) went to the movies. Nearly everyone owned a television set.

Sacramentans still frequented movie palaces in the late 1940s. Filmmakers who still owned the theaters experimented with new screen technology (Cinerama and Cinemascope), and Sacramento theaters like the Senator adapted. On the site of the old Hippodrome, the new Crest Theater had a gala opening in October 1949, hosting stars William Demarest, Kathryn Grayson, and tenor Mario Lanza for the premier of *The Midnight Kiss*. However, movie studios began to unload their branch theaters. Moreover, the popularity of television and the decline in the central business district meant the end of downtown movie palaces. By 1969, historian Andrew Flink notes that only nine theaters still operated in the downtown. Suburban theaters, however, prospered. The Village Theater opened at Fulton and El Camino in late 1949, the Rainbow Theater in Carmichael in the same year. Drive-in theaters too began to dot the landscape. In 1946, the El Rancho Drive-In Theater commenced operation in West Sacramento. In June 1950, the Fruitridge opened its ports to motorists as did the Bell Drive-In on Marysville Road. Others followed.

One development that slowed and even arrested the entertainment exodus from downtown was the Music Circus, a summer stock musical theater providing first-rate entertainment. The prototype premiered in Lambertville, New Jersey where musicals were performed in the round for appreciative audiences in a Chatauqua-like tent. This format came to the attention of two Beverly Hills producers, Russell Lewis and Howard Young, both veterans of Broadway productions. Eleanor McClatchy, Sacramento's chief arts patron, invited the two producers to come to Sacramento and attempt a summer musical theater in the state capital. McClatchy's generous financial backing and Young's and Lewis's expertise made a powerful match, and in 1951 the new Sacramento Light Opera Association was formed and space rented at 15th and H from the Sacramento Civic Repertory. The Music Circus opened its first season with a performance of Jerome Kern's *Showboat*. The audiences, packed into the large flowing tent, grew and grew through the summer, and the Music Circus became a popular summer pastime. Although summer heat and uncomfortable seating sometimes marred the evening's pleasure, steady upgrading of shows, music, and the physical structure assured continued popularity for the summer theater.

More "highbrow" entertainment was provided by the Sacramento Philharmonic Orchestra, conducted for years by Fritz Berens. The Saturday Club arranged a cultural season that brought soloists, the San Francisco symphony, and ballet troupes to Sacramento. Annual visits of the San Francisco Opera company brought divas like soprano Leontyne Price to perform in the Memorial Auditorium.

As the 1950s opened, radio was still the predominant medium. Sacramento had five major stations (KFBK, KXOA, KGMS, KCRA, and KROY) with national hookups. Public broadcasting took an important turn in 1944 when advertising executive Ewing C. Kelly formed the Central Valley Broadcasting Company. Working with partners David R. McKinley and C. Vernon Hansen, Kelly made application to the Federal Communications Commission (FCC) for a local 250-watt AM radio station. KCRA began broadcasting in April 1945 as an NBC affiliate, and in 1951 expanded its power. In August 1949, Kelly and Hansen (McKinley was bought out) began an FM station.

However, radio was soon eclipsed by the rise of television. Television had first been demonstrated in Sacramento at the 1947 State Fair when students of the Grant Technical Schools built the first viewer and transmitter in Sacramento County. Sacramentans with high aerials and favorable weather could pick up television broadcasts from San Francisco. Sacramento's first television station, KCCC, opened to great fanfare in 1953, but its signal was weak. In September 1954, KOVR began broadcasting. In March 1955, KBET began broadcasting, and in 1959 changed its title to KXTV. In August 1948, KCRA applied to the FCC for a television station, but was compelled to await approval until 1955.

Howard Young, left, and Russell Lewis consult an ouiji board about next season's prospects and come up all smiles in this caricature by John C. Oglesby of The Bee staff.

Sacramento Bee artist Jack Oglesby sketches a happy Russell Lewis and Howard Young, co-creators of the Music Circus.

YOUTH CULTURE

In 1946, Sacramento's baby boom began when county births soared from 4,236 in 1945 to 5,354. This group and subsequent large "classes" of newborns began to work their way through the Sacramento school system, creating huge changes. A new cohort of young people compelled businesses and public facilities to cater to the youngsters in a variety of ways. William Land Park added Fairy Tale Town, a youngster's attraction in 1959. Entertainment venues for youngsters were added to local theaters, which ran popular matinees of Disney cartoon movies like *Snow White, Sleeping Beauty,* and *Song of the South*. Television broadcasting carved out its own children's hours in the early morning and with after school cartoon shows like KXTV's *Diver Dan* and his puppet pal O-U Squid, and *Captain Delta* on KOVR. The proximity of the airbases made the air force fighter *Captain Sacto* (played by the popular Harry Martin for many years) a natural Sacramento child entertainer. Children's clothing and toy stores like Bob's Toyland appeared with great success.

Sacramento's pop music culture, fed by local youth, evolved with the rest of the state and nation. Locally, teen dancers rocked to the tunes of Bill Rase and others. Local radio station KROY began to spin pop tunes and later KXOA became the button most pushed on car radios by Sacramento teens. In February 1963, Sacramento native Fred Vail brought the newly formed Beach Boys to the Memorial Auditorium. The following year the popular group recorded a live album from the Memorial. A year later, the Rolling Stones rolled into Sacramento to play at the Memorial Auditorium.

Sacramento had its collective anxieties about "wild youth." A particular source of concern was cruising down K Street in a souped-up car or "hot rod." Although discouraged by local police and parent groups, the K Street drag became a popular rite-of-passage. Ministers, PTAs, and other groups worried about the effects of rock music, "suggestive" attire, and movies with the surly images of teen idols such as Elvis Presley, James Dean, and others. Historian William Mahan recalled Marian Stebbins, Dean of Students at Sacramento High School in 1960, expelling every girl who came to school wearing jeans.

The years after World War II completed Sacramento's transformation to a metropolitan center. The city's boundaries were now more fluid than ever as the automobile and freeways created new configurations of population and commercial life. The net effect of the changes seemed to leave the old city behind and transfer energy and vitality to the suburbs. The downtown faded as the shopping centers and theaters of new areas buzzed with life. But the pace of change was only beginning. Sacramento would burst to life again in the final decades of the twentieth century.

7. Urban Renaissance

In the latter years of the twentieth century, Sacramento emerged even more sharply as the hub of a thriving five county metropolitan area. By the end of the century, a new skyscape had emerged dramatically from the flat floor of the Central Valley. The city had weathered significant challenges, especially the loss of federal dollars that had poured into the region through the military installations and the aerospace industry. It had met the sometimes tense social challenges brought about by shifting demographics and was acknowledged by some as a showcase of diversity. Thanks to new leadership, the aging downtown was recreated and the city and its neighborhoods became a sought-after alternative to suburban life. The city itself began to think in regional rather than local concerns. New forms of transportation and communication knit the Sacramento metropolitan area together in a manner vaguely reminiscent of the city's earlier days when Sacramento was a relatively self-contained urban center.

The Challenges of the 1970s

The bright promises of redevelopment and road construction had left a mixed legacy. The new superhighways had united the metropolis and improved transportation significantly. Its aggressive urban redevelopment program had eliminated the worst slums, and high-rise buildings and town houses began to be built where taverns and flophouses once stood. However, all of this had come at a price. Urban neighborhoods in the path of the freeways had been destroyed, and property values of the remaining structures in the vicinity had dropped. Ambitious plans to restore K Street to its role as a shopping center by making it a pedestrian mall had also failed. People had abandoned the downtown, and one wag quipped that one could "roll a bowling ball" down the nearly vacant K Street Mall without hitting anything. Meanwhile, pranksters had taken to filling the fountain at 11th and K with laundry detergent and occasionally someone could be found taking a bath in the suds.

A series of unfortunate incidents in the 1970s further diminished Sacramento's self-esteem. The most traumatic was a tragic air accident in 1972 that sent a Korean War–era aircraft careening across Freeport Boulevard and smashing into the popular Farrell's Ice Cream Parlour, killing 22 people, many of them youngsters. The searing memory of this event—memorialized by a plaque in 2003—cast a pall over the city. In April 1975, members of the violent Symbionese Liberation Army, with heiress Patty Hearst participating, robbed the Crocker Bank in Carmichael and killed Myrna Lee Opsahl, a 42-year-old church worker depositing her congregation's Sunday collection. The perpetrators of these crimes were not brought to justice until 2003. In September of 1975 a visit by President Gerald Ford nearly turned into disaster when Lynne "Squeaky" Fromme, an acolyte of mass murderer Charles Manson, tried to fire a shot at the chief executive. The jarring nature of these events and the discomfort of the future of the downtown laid bare a collective anxiety in Sacramento's citizenry. At the same time, the city's demographics began to change as well.

A CHANGING POPULATION

Sacramento had always hosted an array of ethnic groups and communities. However, community leaders had continually pressed newcomers to "Americanize." This emphasis, combined with the relative proximity of ethnic neighborhoods (Sacramento never had the self-contained ethnic enclaves typical of many other American cities), had tended to homogenize the city.

Filipinos constituted one of the first waves of Sacramento's ethnic identity. Young, single Filipino men had been coming to Sacramento since the 1920s. Attracted by the prospect of jobs as farm laborers, they lived in the West End where

The Farrell's Ice Cream Parlour tragedy in September 1972 spawned new rules for pilots and airports.

141

employment agencies recruited them. After World War II, more Filipinos moved to the state capital—so much so that in 1961, Sacramento and the Philippine capital of Manila became sister cities. In December of that year, Sacramento mayor James B. McKinney declared December 28 "Jose Rizal Day" in honor of the Filipino nationalist hero who had been executed by the Spanish 65 years earlier. (Rizal had actually visited Sacramento in 1888 and expressed admiration for the harmony that existed among various ethnic groups.) The locus of the Filipino community was the Catholic Church. A group of Filipino Sisters had come to Sacramento in the 1950s and had begun to organize cultural and religious celebrations. After 1965, there was a huge increase in Sacramento's Filipino community.

Filipinos came because immigration laws were changed. In 1965, Congress revised the immigration legislation of the 1920s and removed nationality and race as a basis for inclusion or exclusion from the United States. They also eliminated ethnic quotas. The new law placed a priority on the family as the unit of immigration. At the same time, American society experienced a revival of interest in the preservation of ethnicity. Sacramento had to learn a new way of accommodating immigrants. Among the newcomers were thousands of southeast Asian families dislocated by the Vietnam War. After the collapse of South Vietnam in 1975, Sacramento welcomed thousands of Vietnamese, Laotians (Mien), and Hmong to the city. By 1995, there were over 40,000 Vietnamese living in

Mary Gorre is crowned queen of the Filipino community during the Philippine Independence Day celebration, 1946.

Sacramento. By 2000, from 18,000 to 25,000 Hmong resided in the county, and by 2002, over 12,000 Mien also lived in the region. Jobs and educational opportunities, especially in the high-tech and medical fields, attracted scores of Indians and Pakistanis as well. Stockton Boulevard, a declining commercial corridor leading south from the city, sprouted into new life as Chinese, Vietnamese, Filipino, and Hmong Sacramentans bought homes and opened businesses along a 24-mile stretch from 14th Avenue to Morrison Creek.

The new cultural diversity reflected itself in places of worship. Sikhs and Hindus came from the Indian subcontinent. Muslims had been in Sacramento since the 1890s, and with an influx of Pakistani immigrants, Sacramento had one of the first mosques on the West Coast by the 1940s. Korean and Vietnamese Catholics built their own churches in the 1980s. Russian families arrived in Sacramento, building on communities across the river in Bryte. Pentecostal and other evangelical churches flourished as radio evangelists played a role in bringing thousands of Ukrainians. By 1995, over 20,000 Ukrainians lived in the Sacramento area.

GOVERNMENTAL CHANGE

The growing ethnic diversity of the city began to reflect itself in politics. Sacramento city government reached a crossroads of sorts by the end of the 1960s. The general political ferment of the period had brought to the fore a new group of leaders, many of them representatives of the city's diverse ethnic pool. In 1965, Sun Wong was elected to office, the first Chinese American in the city's history. Two years later, attorney Milton McGhee, the first African American took his seat on the board, and in 1969 the rising tide of Latino voters elected Manuel Ferrales to office. In this social cauldron, citizens mobilized to create a more responsive and updated city government. One such group, the "Citizens for Better Government," took aim at the 1921 City Charter and proposed a series of reforms that they thought would make the city more responsive to the shifting needs and changing demographics of Sacramento. They urged, among other things, the creation of voting districts for city council members (replacing the at-large election that had kept the City Council largely a bastion of white, middle-class males) and the at-large election of an independent mayor. Carefully saved, however, was the heart of the 1921 reform: the post of city manager. Whatever the other changes of city government, its city managers, including Richard Rathfon, Walter Slipe, William Edgar, and Robert Thomas, continued to exercise a powerful influence on the shape of Sacramento public life.

These reform proposals worked their way through supporters on the existing city council and voters approved them in a November 1970 election. Eight new council posts were created, each elected by separate districts, and an at-large mayor was approved. The new city council included one incumbent, Manuel Ferrales, but also welcomed a host of newcomers such as Anne Rudin, Philip Isenberg, Robert Matsui, Rosenwald Robinson, R. Burnett Miller, and Ritz Naygrow. Richard Marriott, a pro-labor activist, was elected mayor.

Attorney Milton McGhee, shown here in October 1974, became the first African American to serve on the city council.

The mayor's position evolved dramatically during this time. While mayors of the 1960s were highly visible figures popular with the city's business elite, the mayors of the closing decades of the twentieth century cut more dynamic figures as movers and shakers. Mayor Philip Isenberg, who took over after Marriott resigned in 1975, helped shape the mayor's position into a major political force. But the two dueling politicos that most strongly affected the tide of city government were Anne Rudin and Joe Serna Jr. Rudin was elected mayor in 1983 and served until 1992—not the first woman to hold that office but the first woman elected directly to the mayor's job by Sacramento voters. When Isenberg departed city government for the legislature, Rudin and Serna competed to dominate city government. Both were ambitious politicians, eager to play a role in developing Sacramento life. Rudin was more of a political and social liberal, opposed to war, openly supportive of socially liberal causes such as gay and lesbian rights. To the consternation of many, she openly speculated that Sacramento might be able to survive without the presence of its three major military installations. Serna was less easy to characterize. His base of support came from the growing number of Latino Sacramentans and organized labor. He cut his political teeth on his work with farm labor organizer Cesar Chavez. But Serna was above all a pragmatist, willing to make deals with ideological opponents to advance the cause of Sacramento's civic and economic health.

Sacramento's public officials faced a lot of issues from the 1970s on. Perhaps the single most important was the pace and scope of urban growth. This pitted developers, anxious to take advantage of new land and new markets and expand aggressively, against those who proposed a more orderly phased-in approach. The latter group continually warned against the "Los Angelization" of Sacramento—meaning ill-planned urban sprawl. This faction had Rudin's support. Serna by contrast, a protege of former Mayor Isenberg, who had appointed him to the City Redevelopment Board, favored a more aggressive approach to growth and change. A careful politician, Serna was not willing to align himself too openly with the pro-development group, but clearly believed that the future of Sacramento required more boldness and risk-taking than he thought Rudin was willing to provide.

In the 1980s, the signal issue focused on the section of land called North Natomas, a 9,000-acre strip of farmland between Sacramento and the Metropolitan Airport. Since it was located within a natural flood plain, Sacramento's master plan had insisted that this area remain agricultural and not be subdivided for other uses. Developers wanted to open it for growth, and they had secured important backing from the county. In order to get the city to agree to re-zone the land for development, developers dangled the bait of a major sports

In 1969, the rising tide of Latino voters elected Manuel Ferrales, shown here in October 1974, to the city council. (Photo by Rudolfo Cueller.)

stadium—something that appealed to a wide spectrum of Sacramentans. The issue of North Natomas figured largely in the 1983 mayoral campaign between Anne Rudin and florist Ross Relles. Rudin, who urged slow growth in the area, barely won against the less-experienced Relles. In 1985, developers Greg Lukenbill and Joseph and Richard Benvenuti forced the city's hand when they purchased a National Basketball Association team, the Kansas City Kings, and completed a 10,000 seat arena just east of the North Natomas land. Swept away by the public support for the Sacramento Kings and the prospect of professional sports in Sacramento, the city council ignored Rudin's objections and approved the re-zoning. A second arena holding over 18,000 fans was then built to accommodate the surging fans in the area.

Serna's turn for city governance came when Rudin turned down a third term in 1992. Easily besting a host of competitors, Serna, long a veteran of city politics, plunged into the task of governing the city, putting his brand of aggressive leadership to work. Although the mayor had no power over local schools, he nonetheless waded into the middle of contentious school district politics by pressing for improvements in the public schools, which had some of the worst drop-out rates in the state. Attempting to build on the success of the Kings, he worked aggressively to court other sports teams, seeking professional football and baseball franchises for the city. To attract businesses to relocate to Sacramento, he helped put together an expensive incentive package for the Packard Bell Company to take over the old Army Depot. Serna celebrated the increased cultural diversity of the city not only by his own ethnicity but by creating the popular Festival of the Family, replacing the more staid Camellia Festival that was to his mind a relic of the old Sacramento elite. Serna died in November 1999 and was succeeded by interim mayor Jimmy Yee. A spirited campaign waged in 2000 brought the election of Heather Fargo, Sacramento's third woman mayor. At the same time, Sacramento approved the creation of a full-time mayor's position.

The election of Anne Rudin and Heather Fargo also placed a spotlight on the evolving role of women in Sacramento life. In 1960, thanks largely to the air bases and the expansion of state government, Sacramento had one of the highest percentages of women in the workforce in California. A variety of women's clubs and organizations had always created a sphere of influence for Sacramento women, but in the latter twentieth century, the somewhat generic women's clubs gave way to professional organizations such as the League of Women Voters, the American Association of University Women, and various political clubs. Three very powerful women helped shape Sacramento culture in the 1950s and 1960s: Eleanor McClatchy, head of the *Bee*, Marion Armstrong, president of Weinstock's, and Lucy Ritter, vice president of Cal-Western Life Insurance Company. As the general consciousness of women's issues and status increased in the 1960s and 1970s, Sacramento women became more visible in "traditional" male bastions such as state and local government, fire fighting, and law enforcement, as well as in sports and the legal profession. In 2001, Sacramento ranked high in women-owned businesses. Political agitation by such groups as Grandmothers for Peace highlighted the role of

Eleanor McClatchy, president of McClatchy newspapers for more than 40 years, helped shape Sacramento culture in the 1950s and 1960s.

women in a military city. Barriers to women's advance such as the "males only" policy of the Sutter Club came under fire. Politicians like Sandra Smoley, Muriel Johnson, Illa Collins, and Deborah Ortiz assumed prominent positions in local and state government, and gender-equity issues moved more prominently into Sacramento public life.

THE DECLINE OF OLD INDUSTRIES AND BASE CLOSURES

Toward the end of the twentieth century, Sacramento's economy changed decisively. Earlier economic mainstays, the railroad and the canneries, went the way of all flesh. The rail yards had been waning since the 1930s. In 1937, the last locomotive rolled off the lines, and the rail shops turned to the maintenance of large diesel engines. The decline of the railroads had begun. Fewer and fewer people took the train, opting for airplane or automobile travel. In addition, the re-shifting of management and the relocation of facilities eventually spelled an end to the longtime service of the shops. The Western Pacific closed its shops on Sutterville Road about 1960. In 1979, Southern Pacific car repairs were transferred to the rail yards in Roseville. By 1981, the Sacramento Locomotive Works, as the shops had been retitled, began to shrink in size and labor force. The acquisition of the Southern Pacific by the Union Pacific temporarily staved off closure, but by 1999, the Sacramento yards were too old and the demands of centralized corporate management required change; the yards closed, leaving behind acres of highly toxic soil. Clean-up progresses today, and eventually the yards and the adjoining depot and storage areas may be the site of major new urban development.

Sacramento's canning industry, once an economic mainstay, began to decline as well. Sacramento's four major packing plants were hit by the twin blows of improved technology and decreasing consumer demand. Canning technology became more and more mechanized, requiring fewer workers. Likewise, the development of frozen foods seriously undercut the longtime popularity of canned goods. Consumer demand further declined when health-conscious consumers began to prefer fresh fruits and vegetables and shied away from preservation processes that added calories and robbed fruits and vegetables of their vitamins. Libby, McNeil & Libby closed their plant on C Street in 1980, followed by Del Monte in 1981. Even the huge Bercut-Richards plant on Seventh and Richards folded in the early 1980s. The only remnants of the once thriving food processing industry were the Campbell Soup plant on Franklin Boulevard and the Blue Diamond Almond Growers Cooperative off 16th Street.

But the biggest change in Sacramento's economy came with the closure of its three military bases that had been in the region since the 1930s and 1940s. The unsteady reliance on federal dollars had first been felt when Aerojet General, a private company depending heavily on federal contracts, began to experience substantial declines in the sale of propulsion systems for the Titan, Minuteman, and Polaris missiles in 1965. From its peak employment of 22,000, the aerospace giant began laying off employees until by 1972 only 9,539 worked at the plant. Military installations seemed safe during the Vietnam conflict. However, national pressures brought on by the growing peace movement and the wind-down of the Vietnam War during the Nixon administration brought the three Sacramento facilities under the microscope of federal budget-cutters. Already in the 1970s rumors had been floating that McClellan Air Force Base was slated to close. Mather Field appeared on a "hit list" of possible closures in 1987, but vigorous efforts by Congressmen Vic Fazio and Robert Matsui stalled the decision. But in 1988, Congress created the Base Realignment and Closure Commission (BRAC), an independent agency that evaluated the need for military bases and made recommendations to the secretary of defense. By late 1988, the commission had placed Mather on its list, and in 1993 the base closed permanently.

The end of the Cold War in 1989 created additional pressure for a "peace dividend" that included reduced defense expenditures. Secretary of Defense Richard Cheney proposed a series of base closures and consolidations, many of them targeting California bases and among them the Sacramento Army Depot with its 3,498 jobs. In June 1991, the commission voted to shutter the depot. Some of its jobs were transferred to other places. Some were permanently eliminated. With extensive city help, the buildings were made available to Packard Bell.

McClellan Field braced for the worst, and in 1993 its name appeared on the dreaded list. However, here the fight to save the field was more intense. Sacramentans attempted to work creatively with BRAC to build a case for McClellan's ongoing existence. Mayor Serna and Chamber of Commerce

148

President Thomas Eres lobbied incessantly to keep the base open. But their efforts and those of area congressmen were in vain. On June 22, 1995, BRAC voted to close McClellan, and the base slowly faded, closing permanently in April 2001.

Government efforts to help during the transition were considerable. In addition to the standard option of job relocation, workers from McClellan and elsewhere were given training for new positions. The lands and buildings of the military bases were turned over to local government and to private industry for development. Mather retained the Veteran's Hospital and McClellan the base exchange (BX) for the benefit of the numerous military retirees in the area. Two thousand acres of Mather became a county-run airport used by air-cargo firms. Another 2,000 acres were transformed into a regional park. McClellan also transitioned much of its 8.5 million square feet of space to private sector purposes. County officials worked closely with private development and created McClellan Business Park, a mixed-use complex of office space and industrial facilities.

HIGH TECH AND STATE GOVERNMENT

The departure of these three bases and the precipitous decline in the once strong aerospace industry dealt Sacramento a blow in her solar plexus. The ripple effect of the departures and job losses on schools, businesses, churches, and the security of community life created apprehension and tension. Fortunately, state government jobs remained stable and a new economic mainstay, the computer

Mayor Joseph A. Serna Jr. pressed hard to improve the city's public schools and worked aggresssively to attract new businesses to Sacramento.

industry, appeared, helping to replace the bread and butter jobs that created Sacramento and continued the city's reputation for economic solidity.

The computer chip technology that had transformed the Silicon Valley of California in the 1970s found its way to the Sacramento metropolitan area in the spring of 1978 when Alan L. Seely, an executive for Hewlett Packard, opened a plant in Roseville. Hewlett Packard began operation in 1980 and soon became one of the top ten employers in the Sacramento region. Other computer-manufacturing firms came to Roseville, including Shugart Electronics, a Sunnyvale-based firm, and Japanese-owned NEC. Intel built a plant in Folsom, Apple in Laguna, and Oracle in Rocklin. The hi-tech revolution of the 1980s and 1990s brought scores of highly-trained and well-paid employees to the region as the demand for personal computers skyrocketed.

State government continued to grow. Even with conservative Republican governors at the helm, the number of people required to keep the state government functional escalated. Bright young professionals continued to move to the capital in the 1970s and 1980s—some of them attracted by the quirky liberalism of Governor Jerry Brown (1975–1983). These new state workers and reorganized agencies soon began to demand new office space and more up-to-date communications technology. New state office buildings for the Environmental Protection Agency, the Justice Department, and the Departments of Education and Health Services were built in the downtown, causing the town to buzz with life during the day. State workers also played a role in urging a revivification of the city's night life, dining options, and public entertainment. Likewise, scores of lobbyists anxious to press their causes set up shop in the growing number of capital office buildings. They too resided in city neighborhoods and pressed city leaders to make Sacramento a first-class capital city through the provision of social amenities such as theater, restaurants, and other forms of recreation.

Among the evolving venues of city life was the city's media establishment. The long domination of the *Sacramento Bee* continued even after the death of Eleanor McClatchy in 1980. When the *Bee* switched from its long-standing evening format to a morning edition, the rival *Union*'s days were numbered. In 1994, the *Union* finally gave up the ghost. Already in 1978 Eleanor McClatchy's nephew Charles K. (also known as C.K. like his grandfather) had taken over as president of the family company. Young McClatchy made significant changes in the business, pulling the company out of its television and radio ventures and buying smaller newspapers in growing cities like Tacoma, Anchorage, and Minneapolis. In 1988, the McClatchy company went public and issued stocks. Young C.K. died unexpectedly in 1989 and Erwin Potts became the first non-family member to head McClatchy Company. In 1999, the company's revenues exceeded $1 billion.

BRINGING THE SUBURBS TO THE CITY

New state workers and lobbyists anxious to live near their jobs and suburbanites anxious for a break from their cul-de-sacs and malls looked for ways to make

Sacramento more socially appealing. With public and private initiatives, Sacramento took on a new look. In effect, as one developer noted, Sacramento transferred many of the appealing features of the suburbs to the city. Likewise, a renewed appreciation for the charm of the old city's architecture, its tree-shaded streets and its convenience helped to re-shape the city's appeal. Sacramentans rediscovered the charm of some its old buildings. Old Sacramento's transformation from skid row to a tourist area was sealed in 1976 with the building of the California State Railroad Museum in the old town. As well, popular sites like the docked *Delta King* riverboat provided dining and light theater entertainment.

Sacramento's most visible public building, the state capitol, also came in for major renovations. A 1972 seismic study revealed that the venerable old structure was unsafe. In 1976, a major renovation was undertaken, which rebuilt and retrofitted the capitol from the basement up, reusing original materials or carefully reproducing historical replicas. While the legislature met in temporary buildings to the rear of the capitol, the $67.7 million project proceeded ahead, finally opening to the public in 1982.

The destruction of the 1927 movie palace, the Alhambra Theater, and its replacement with a Safeway market, roused Sacramentans from their torpor. The theater tumbled to the wrecker's ball in 1972 after the public voted against a bond

A major renovation of the state capitol was undertaken in 1976.

measure to preserve it. In reaction to that failure, many Sacramentans mobilized to preserve some of their past. In 1973, the Sacramento branch of the American Association of University Women issued *Vanishing Victorians: A Guide to the Historic Homes of Sacramento*. This popular history of Sacramento's elegant old Victorian homes played a role in awakening Sacramentans to their architectural heritage and arresting the destruction of historic city buildings. The Sacramento Old City Association was then formed to preserve the city's architectural heritage. This association and young government staffers who came to Sacramento during the term of Governor Jerry Brown took a new interest in rehabbing old homes and in snapping up inexpensive properties in midtown—an area that had been virtually redlined by insurance companies. Thanks in part to the increasing congestion on Sacramento freeways, the efforts of vocal neighborhood associations, and successful efforts to alter busy traffic patterns in residential neighborhoods all over Sacramento, a new interest in gentrification developed that revived the downtown area. Midtown properties, along with those in Land Park and Curtis Park, soon became premium locations.

In 1976, the downtown received a boost when a long-awaited Sacramento Community Center opened its doors. The huge complex sprawled south from J to L Street and included a major meeting hall, breakout rooms, and other amenities. Later additions included a theater and symphony hall. The community center created renewed interest in the renovation of K Street that had been discussed

The Downtown Plaza opened in October 1993, adding to the revitalization efforts.

during the early phases of urban renewal. Despite the creation of a pedestrian mall, the once thriving commercial street and adjoining J Street had little foot traffic and businesses attracted little more than the noontime luncheon crowds. The offending "tank traps" were torn out and a new mall emerged. The centerpiece was an 18-mile modern light rail system completed in 1987, shuttling commuters from Sacramento's northern suburbs to the downtown. Subsequent stops moved southward with proposed plans to link the entire region by this highly popular form of mass transit. Around the downtown, two new hotels (a modern Hyatt Regency on the corner of 12th and L and a new Sheraton, using the facade of the Public Market on J Street and 12th, designed by architect Julia Morgan in the 1920s, as its lobby entrance) set the stage for making Sacramento a convention center.

Malls had become the defining points of suburban Sacramento and city developers sought to bring the more attractive aspects of the suburban malls downtown. In 1989, the Downtown Plaza Associates took a fresh look at the plight of the lonely Macy's and Weinstock stores that had been planted at the opposite end of K Street in 1960. Ernest Hahn of the Hahn Company of San Diego floated a bold plan by architect Louis Jerde to expand the shopping area at the foot of K Street by 250,000 square feet and to build an outdoor plaza with ample parking, food and theater concessions, and a medley of specialty shops designed to bring people in from the suburbs. The $157 million plan went forward and in October 1993 the Downtown Plaza opened with a gala bash. Predicted Sacramento councilwoman Deborah Ortiz, "If anything is going to turn around the Sacramento revenue base, this is it." Old Sacramento was connected to the Plaza Mall by a tunnel, which included a history wall that displayed the names and faces of many of Sacramento's movers and shakers from various eras.

Sacramento sprouted a skyline in the 1980s and 1990s. In addition to a host of new state government buildings, city developers helped to build an array of new office space for the growing downtown workforce and for cultural needs. The 28-story Renaissance Tower was built in 1989. Behind the city library an expansive Galleria named for local developer Angelo Tsakapoulous provided a venue for library-sponsored lectures and social events. An addition to the library included the establishment of a room devoted solely to Sacramento history. A much-needed refurbishing of the old city hall and a major extension of its facilities was commenced in 2003. Across from the city hall, Plaza Park was renamed in honor of labor activist Cesar Chavez and decorative banners, new sidewalks, and refurbished fountains made it a favored spot for transients, residents, and downtown employees.

Older buildings in the downtown underwent extensive renovation. In 1992, joint public and private efforts spared the Memorial Auditorium from demolition and underwrote a major restoration of the "Old Barn." Re-opened to great acclaim in November 1996, the modernized Memorial Auditorium continued to be a popular site for concerts, some indoor athletic events, graduations, and public ceremonies. In 2003, California governor Gray Davis held his inauguration ceremonies in the auditorium. Major renovations of the city's stately Cathedral of the Blessed Sacrament began in the summer of 2003. Around the cathedral,

Sacramentans enjoyed a popular weekly street fair on Thursday nights on K Street from Memorial Day through the summer. Later, the venue was reduced to a more manageable outdoor market.

The beginning of the summer holidays were marked by another popular Sacramento event, the Jazz Jubilee. This important festival was spearheaded by a group of local musicians who formed the New Sacramento Traditional Jazz Society in 1968. The group won public visibility when they organized a jazz concert to support the rehabilitation of the *Delta King*, anchored along Front Street in Old Sacramento, in 1969. Nearly 4,000 turned out for the concert, and with good organization the group managed to put on a jazz festival in 1974, modeled after successful ones in Monterey and Newport, Rhode Island. Almost 3,000 showed up for this event held on Memorial Day weekend, and in every subsequent year the numbers attending grew, as did the number of bands. Originally the festival highlighted Dixieland, but by 1992 a wide array of musical styles (Gospel, Latin, Zydeco, Blues, and even Barbershop) were added to the popular medley of performers. Nearly 100,000 attended the festival in 1992.

Movie going picked up again in the 1970s and 1980s, spearheaded by a number of exciting feature films that found new fans. The new customers found that films in a theater had significant advantage over television or even the later popular video rental stores. In 1967, the dome-shaped Century Theaters opened near Arden Fair Mall. The comfortable seating and the tiered rows provided comfort and an unobstructed view for moviegoers. A new downtown theater attracting much attention was the big-screen technology called IMAX that became the chief venue of the newly reconditioned Esquire Theater on K Street. Using the marquee of the old theater that had long since closed, the Esquire combined the nostalgic memory of old Sacramento with the technology of the new.

One development that kept Sacramentans coming downtown was the popular Music Circus. The familiar Music Circus tent had undergone a major expansion and improvement for the 1968–1969 season. However, it could still be a hot and sticky experience, especially for the entertainers who worked under the lights, as well as for unlucky patrons who occasionally found themselves sitting near the huge tent poles that obstructed their view of the stage. After battles with its neighbors, Music Circus leaders managed to secure permission for a new parking structure and tent facility. Sponsored by Wells Fargo, the Music Circus's new pavilion premiered in the summer of 2003 and included comfortable seating, better air conditioning, and more rest rooms to remove whatever discomfort may have been a part of this now familiar Sacramento institution. The demand for Broadway productions apart from the summer season was met with a popular Broadway Series begun by the Light Opera Association at the Community Center theater in 1989.

SPORTS

Nothing brought people back to Sacramento more successfully than professional sports. Far and away the most popular cultural expansion in Sacramento during this period was the addition of professional sports in the form of a National Basketball Association team.

Although interconnected with the larger issue of the development of North Natomas, the advent of the popular Sacramento Kings is a story in its own right. In 1979, a young 24-year-old local contractor, Greg Lukenbill, teamed with developers Joseph and Richard Benvenuti to propose the building of a 32,500-seat multipurpose stadium and 20,000-seat sports complex in North Natomas. Thwarted for a time by the city's unwillingness to re-zone the area, Luckenbill persevered, formed the Sacramento Sports Association, and in April 1985 purchased the Kansas City Kings. The advent of the Kings launched the building of a new sports arena underwritten by the Atlantic Richfield Company and called ARCO Arena. Lukenbill eventually sold the franchise to Jim Thomas in 1992, and then in January of 1998, the Las Vegas–based Maloof family acquired partial ownership of the team, which then lead to their controlling interest in the team and ARCO Arena the following year. Under the ownership of the Maloof family, the leadership of General Manager Geoff Petrie, and the coaching of Rick Adelman, who joined the club in the 1998–1999 season, the Kings soon emerged as a major NBA play-off team, moving forward to the Conference finals in 2002. Sacramentans thronged Kings games. Kings sports apparel, the hero worship of Kings players, and the economic boost and prestige of the popular team made the Kings one of the defining elements of urban life.

In April 1996, a women's team, the Sacramento Monarchs, premiered at the ARCO as part of the Women's National Basketball Association. Other efforts to

Sacramento's Jazz Jubilee, shown here in May 1975, takes place on Memorial Day weekend and includes a wide array of musical styles.

recruit professional teams to Sacramento were endorsed by Sacramento mayor Joe Serna. Serna hoped to attract the NFL Oakland Raiders to Sacramento. There was also some interest expressed in relocating the Pittsburgh Pirates, owned by Kevin McClatchy, a member of the prominent *Sacramento Bee* family. More realistic voices, however, urged the return of Triple A baseball to Sacramento and the construction of a new park to host games. Arguments between Mayor Serna and local developers over the location of the park ensued, and the city pulled out of the process when a group of local business leaders decided to build the park in West Sacramento rather than on the old rail yard grounds that Serna had pushed. With a generous $8 million from the Raley Company, a new field (Raley Field) opened in April 2000, and a new team (the former Vancouver Canadians), purchased from Japan Sports Systems and renamed the Sacramento River Cats, stepped up to the plate.

The Poor in a Changing Sacramento

Amid the glitter and glamour of the new service and entertainment industries in the downtown, the reality of urban poverty also began to register an imprint on Sacramento. First the gold rush and later the presence of the railroad and the soft winter climate of California brought unemployed transients to the city. However, the demolition of the West End with its cheap flophouses and its day labor market as well as the cutbacks in care for the mentally ill during the administration of Governor Ronald Reagan turned loose a new crop of homeless men, women, and families that roamed the streets of the city, sleeping in alleys, in front of churches, under bridges, and along the riverbank. Efforts to feed the hungry have been a special mission of the religious communities of the area. Private charities such as the Union Rescue Mission and the Salvation Army took the lead in feeding the homeless for many years. In more recent times, the Episcopal and Roman Catholic Churches have taken a more active role in providing food, shelter, and care for the poor. Along 12th Street, a homeless feeding and care center begun by Dan and Chris Delany known as Loaves & Fishes was established by a number of religious groups and has expanded substantially since its fairly modest beginnings in the late 1970s.

★ ★ ★ ★

Sacramento, like any other American city, is still a work in progress. The city continues to improve and expand its urban space; its neighborhoods and still manageable public ambience attract many who are weary of life in the overdeveloped Bay Area and Silicon Valley. Sacramento's reputation for diversity is its proudest boast to this day, as it continues to encourage its multicultural population to work together for the common good. The city above all has never lost any of its "indomitable" spirit. The same forces that allowed the city to defy nature and rise as a major social, economic, and cultural center near two fast rivers still live to define another generation.

BIBLIOGRAPHY

Avella, Steven M. *A History of the Diocese of Sacramento*. Private publication, 2002.

B'Nai Israel, 150. Sacramento: The Congregation, 1999.

Burns, John, et al. *Sacramento: Gold Rush Legacy, Metropolitan Destiny*. Carlsbad: Heritage Media Corporation, 1999.

Bruno, Lloyd. *Old River Town: A Personal History of Sacramento*. Dunsmuir: Suttertown Publishing, 1996.

Cole, Cheryl. *A History of the Japanese Community in Sacramento, 1993–1972*. San Francisco: R and E Research Associates, 1974.

Connolly, Elaine and Dian Self. *Capital Women: An Interpretative History of Women in Sacramento, 1850–1920*. Sacramento: Capital Women's History Project, 1995.

Comstock, Timothy F. *The Sutter Club: One Hundred Years*. Sacramento: Sutter Club, 1989.

Craft, George S. *California State University Sacramento: The First Forty Years: 1947–1987*. Sacramento: The Hornet Foundation, 1987.

Davis, Winfield J. *An Illustrated History of Sacramento County, California*. Chicago: Lewis Publishing, 1890.

Dillon, Richard. *Captain John Sutter: Sacramento Valley's Sainted Sinner*. Santa Cruz: Western Tanager Press, 1967 and 1981.

Eifler, Mark A. *Gold Rush Captialists: Greed and Growth in Sacramento*. Albuquerque: University of New Mexico Press, 2002.

Flink, Andrew. *A Century of Cinema in Sacramento, 1900–2000*. Rancho Cordova, 1999.

Hurtado, Albert. *Indian Survival on the California Frontier*. New Haven: Yale University Press, 1988.

Kelley, Robert. *Battling the Inland Sea: Floods, Public Policy and the Sacramento Valley*. Berkeley: University of California Press, 1989.

Kibbey, Mead, ed. *1853–1854 Sacramento Directory*. Sacramento: California State Library Foundation, 1997.

———, ed. *J. Horace Culver's Sacramento City Directory for the Year 1851*. Sacramento: California State Library Foundation, 2000.

Kleinschmidt, Bruce, et al. *150 Years of Faith: The Stories of Three Trailblazing Sacramento Churches, 1849–1999*. Sacramento: Tri-Church Sesquicentennial Committee, 1999.

Leland, Dorothy Kupcha. *A Short History of Sacramento*. San Francisco: Lexikon, 1989.

Lord, Myrtle Shaw. *A Sacramento Saga*. Sacramento: Sacramento Chamber of Commerce, 1946.

Maeda, Wayne. *Changing Dreams and Treasured Memories: A Story of Japanese Americans in the Sacramento Region*. Sacramento: Sacramento Japanese Citizens League, 2000.

McGowan Joseph A. and Terry Willis. *Sacramento: Heart of the Golden State*. Woodland Hills: Windsor Publications, 1983.

McGowan Joseph, A. *History of the Sacramento Valley*. 3 vols. New York and West Palm Beach: Lewis Historical Publishing, 1961.

Mims, Julie Elizabeth and Kevin Michael Mims. *Sacramento: A Pictorial History of California's Capital*. Virginia Beach: The Donning Company, 1981.

Morse, John F. *The First History of Sacramento City*. Sacramento: Sacramento Book Collectors Club, 1945.

Neasham, V. Aubrey and James E. Henley. *The City of the Plain*. Sacramento: Sacramento Pioneer Foundation/Sacramento Historic Landmarks Commission, 1969.

Ottley, Alan, ed. *The Sutter Family and the Origins of Gold Rush Sacramento*. Norman: University of Oklahoma Press, 2002.

Owens, Kenneth N., ed. *John Sutter and a Wider West*. Lincoln and London: University of Nebraska Press, 1994.

Pierini, Bruce. *The Italians of Sacramento*. Sacramento: Sacramento County Historical Society, 1997.

Reed, Walter G., ed. *History of Sacramento County*. Los Angeles: Historic Record Company, 1923.

Rogers, Richard C. *The First 100 Years of Sacramento City Schools, 1854–1954*. Sacramento: California Retired Teachers Association/Sacramento Branch, 1991.

Rodgerson, Eleanor. *Adobe, Brick and Steel: A History of Hospitals and Shelters for the Sick in Sacramento and El Dorado Counties*. Sacramento: Sacramento–El Dorado County Medical Society, 1993.

Sacramento Guide Book. Sacramento Bee, 1939.

Severson, Thor. *Sacramento: An Illustrated History: 1839–1874*. Fifth ed. San Francisco: California Historical Society, 1973.

Smith, Jesse M., ed. *Sketches of Old Sacramento*. Sacramento: Sacramento County Historical Society, 1976.

Sutherland, Ruth Ward. *". . . for the people": The Story of SMUD*. Sacramento: Sacramento Municipal Utilities District, 1973.

Willis, William L. *History of Sacramento County*. Los Angeles: Historic Record Company, 1913.

Wilson, Burt. *A History of Sacramento Jazz, 1948–1966*. Canoga Park: Burt Wilson, 1986.

Woolridge, Jesse W. *History of the Sacramento Valley*. Chicago: Pioneer Historical Publishing, 1931.

Wright, George, ed. *History of Sacramento County*. Berkeley: Howell-North, 1960.

150 Years of the Chinese Presence in California. Sacramento: Sacramento Chinese Culture Foundation, 2001.

INDEX